D1417934

DISCARD

The Flaw in
Japanese Management

Research for Business Decisions, No. 83

Richard N. Farmer, Series Editor

Professor of International Business
Indiana University

Other Titles in This Series

No. 74   *Commercial Banking and Interstate Expansion: Issues, Prospects, and Strategies*   Larry A. Frieder

No. 75   *Telecommuting: The Organizational and Behavioral Effects of Working at Home*   Reagan Mays Ramsower

No. 76   *Management in Post-Mao China: An Insider's View*   Joseph Y. Battat

No. 77   *Frontiers of International Accounting: An Anthology*   Frederick D. S. Choi / Gerhard Mueller

No. 79   *Managing God's Organization: The Catholic Church in Society*   Scott Safranski

No. 81   *Troubled Debt Restructuring: An Alternative to Bankruptcy?*   John Hamer

No. 84   *The Impact of Cybernation Technology on Black Automotive Workers in the U.S.*   Samuel D. K. James

The Flaw in Japanese Management

by
Haruo Takagi

UMI RESEARCH PRESS
Ann Arbor, Michigan

Pfeiffer Library
Pfeiffer College
Misenheimer, N. C. 28109

DISCARD

122886

Copyright © 1985, 1984
Haruo Takagi
All rights reserved

Produced and distributed by
UMI Research Press
an imprint of
University Microfilms International
A Xerox Information Resources Company
Ann Arbor, Michigan 48106

Library of Congress Cataloging in Publication Data

Takagi, Haruo, 1949-
　The flaw in Japanese management.

　(Research for business decisions ; no. 83)
　"A revision of author's Ph.D. thesis, Harvard
University, 1984"—T.p. verso.
　Bibliography: p.
　Includes index.
　1. Industrial management—Japan—Case studies.
2. Quality of work life—Japan—Case studies.
3. Employee motivation—Japan—Case studies.　4. Job
security—Japan—Case studies.　I. Title.　II. Series.
HD70.J3T25　1985　　　658'.00952　　　　　85-20832
ISBN 0-8357-1718-6 (alk. paper)

Contents

List of Figures   *vii*

Acknowledgments   *ix*

1   Introduction   *1*

2   The General Framework   *5*
      Literature about Integration between the Individual
         and the Organization
      Literature Review
      Present Research Status
      Formation of the General Framework
      The General Framework

3   Methodology   *23*
      Exploration
      Design
      Process
      Overview

4   The Company   *29*
      The Quarter-Century Study Period: 1957-82
      Organizational Structure
      Human Resources
      The Ranking System

5   The Engineers at the Early-Career Stage: 1957-66   *39*
      Entrance
      Introductory Education and First Placement
      Task Assignment Situations in the R&D Lab

Task Assignment Situations in the Lighting Division Group
Task Assignment Situations in the Small Appliances Division Group
Transfers
Outcomes

6   The Engineers at the Mid-Career Stage: 1967-78   *53*
Promotion to the Section Manager Level
Task Assignment Situations in the R&D Lab
Task Assignment Situations in the Lighting Division Group
Task Assignment Situations in the Small Appliances Division Group
Transfers at the Section Manager Level
Outcomes

7   The Engineers at the Late-Career Stage: 1979-82   *71*
Promotion to the Department Manager Level
Task Assignment Situations in the R&D Lab
Task Assignment Situations in the Lighting Division Group
Task Assignment Situations in the Small Appliances Division Group
Outcomes

8   Conclusions and Implications   *85*
Conclusions
Implications for Research
Implications for Management Practices

Appendix A   Interview Guide: High-Ranking Manager   *97*

Appendix B   Interview Guide: Research Subject   *99*

Notes   *101*

Bibliography   *105*

Index   *107*

List of Figures

1. Standards for Redesigning the Organization   *7*

2. Career Issues   *10*

3. A Comparison of Five Studies of Integration between the Individual and the Organization   *12*

4. The General Framework   *20*

5. Information and Its Sources   *27*

6. Nominal GNP and Real Growth Rate in Japan   *30*

7. Sales and Profit before Taxes at Tokyo Electric Company, Ltd.   *30*

8. The Ranking System   *34*

9. A Summary of Mutual Expectations between the Individual and the Organization under Lifetime Employment   *91*

Acknowledgments

A number of people have generously and constructively helped me develop this work over the past two and a half years.

First, I would like to thank the engineers who served as research subjects in the study and other managers who cooperated by supplying research information at Tokyo Electric Co., Ltd. (a disguised name). Without their help this study would not have been possible. I am also grateful to Jay Lorsch and Michael Yoshino of Harvard University and Hideo Ishida of Keio University for their academic stimulation and emotional encouragement.

I express special appreciation to Marian Maroney, who, with extraordinary skill, has edited my English writing of this book through several versions. My appreciation also goes to Keio University Education and Research Foundation and Takahashi Industry and Economy Research Foundation, which partially supported my research trip between the U.S.A. and Japan.

I am deeply indebted to Keio University's Masahide Sekimoto, who is my mentor and gave me encouragement throughout my doctoral program, and to Ichiro Kataoka, who supported me in entering this program. Finally, I would like to mention my wife, Yukiko, and two children, Gentaro and Ikuno, for their warm help while I was working in the program.

1

Introduction

This book is aimed at exploring lifetime employment relationships and interactions between a large Japanese company and its members.[1] In particular, its purpose is to better understand the process of the individual's career development and integration with the organization under the unique conditions of lifetime employment.[2]

Originally, I was intrigued by the concept of attaining integration between the individual and the organization to the benefit of both parties. This research interest focused ultimately on Japanese companies because I am a Japanese student of organizational behavior with many opportunities for contact with Japanese executives.

Interviews with these executives and previously developed research evidence suggest that the popular belief that Japanese lifetime employment and its related systems of human resource management promote high integration (Ouchi 1981, "Theory Z") may not be entirely accurate. To develop a better understanding of the effects of lifetime employment on integration between the individual and the organization, I applied an exploratory method of research. There are currently relatively few in-depth studies of "Japanese management," although this term is already in the jargon of researchers and practitioners of management.

A classic issue in the area of organizational behavior is how the individual and the organization can be integrated for the simultaneous attainment of their needs. This is clearly a critical question to the well-being of both parties. In order to insure maximum organizational success, organizations must cope with attracting individuals, holding them within the system, and ensuring their effective performance. On the other hand, individuals in the organization naturally strive to achieve their own personal objectives and are not necessarily committed to attaining organizational goals. Unless the individual and the organization are integrated in some way, the individual's activities required to attain organizational objectives may not coincide with his personal needs. Such activities might be performed half-heartedly and inefficiently and consume many organizational resources.

According to Ouchi's "Theory Z," Japanese companies are advantageous for integration. It explains that lifetime employment and its related personnel practices (such as long-term, seniority-based evaluation and promotion, and nonspecialized career paths) develop an organizational culture in which all members have close and trusting relationships and the ability to communicate complex and subtle subjects. High member involvement and loyalty are facilitated, and effective coordination for complex decision making and conflict resolution can be achieved in this culture.

Furthermore, the theory asserts that the Japanese organizational culture fosters a willingness among employees to accept the long-term equity of the exchange of member contributions for corporate rewards. Individual members' wishes in career development are often sacrificed for the overall maximization of the firm's profitability. In return, members will be repaid in the future through the guarantee of lifetime security and seniority-based reward systems.

As will be seen in chapter 2, integration between the individual and the organization is basically understood as a relationship of exchange for mutual satisfaction throughout the process of career development. So, "Theory Z" states that the two parties are integrated by the exchange of the employee's present performance contribution with the deferred rewards offered by the company throughout the career development process under lifetime employment. Members' trust in this exchange leads to high integration through high involvement and productivity.

However, my preliminary study indicates that many executives in large Japanese companies believe that lifetime employment does not always generate the high involvement among employees as predicted in "Theory Z." In their firms, there are actually a substantial number of employees who use their loyalty to the company to ensure job security while giving only a minimal commitment to their jobs. In fact, this passivity which is often observed under the conditions of lifetime employment is commonly referred to in Japan as the "Large Company Disease."

Two studies support this belief. Yoshino (1968) indicates, in his study of Japanese managerial practices and corporate environment, that "observant senior executives in a number of firms candidly admitted that many highly capable and motivated young men lost their initial enthusiasm as they became affected by what one executive described as the 'tepid' environment" (p. 226). He found a resulting tendency for the guarantee against dismissal and the seniority-based reward system to breed a feeling of complacency among employees.

Another study (Takezawa, 1975) suggests that seniority-based pay and promotion systems under lifetime employment may not be uniformly effective motivators. Takezawa presents evidence of diverse and conflicting values among the different generations of employees in Japan. Younger employees seek more responsible jobs and higher salaries as a result of increased educational experiences. Some middle-aged employees feel threatened because their earnings and compensation benefits do not increase as fast as they previously did. Older employees with greater life expectancies have become more sensitive to job security. Therefore, with these diverse employee values in one Japanese company, long-term promotion and compensation systems seem unable to uniformly attract employees and stimulate their active involvement in the organization.

The implications of these studies encouraged me to conduct a research project to develop a better understanding of the effects of lifetime employment on integration between the individual and the organization. An exploratory method was applied partly because "Theory Z" focused mainly on American companies which Ouchi asserts employ the so-called Japanese management style, and is based on limited empirical data from Japanese companies.

Furthermore, there are currently relatively few intensive exploratory field studies that provide a detailed understanding of the on-going Japanese style of management in individual organizations. To my knowledge, Rohlen (1974) and Clark (1979) provide the only published examples of field research in Japanese companies, and their studies are, respectively, anthropological and sociological, not addressed directly to practicing managers. Although this research methodology cannot test hypotheses, it does generate ideas for people who are concerned with the Japanese style of management.

With multiple methods of data collection, I made a study in 1982 of one large Japanese manufacturing company (Tokyo Electric Company, Ltd.).[3] I closely examined how 27 engineers, who were 44-49 years old, had developed their careers in that company under the lifetime employment system and what integrating relationship had grown between each individual member and the organization. Sources of data were interview notes, personnel records, organization manuals and charts, company newspapers, annual reports, and the book of corporate history published by the company.

As shown later, the general framework was used to examine employees' task assignment situations from their entry into the organization to present, and to understand how they had been motivated in these situations to perform their tasks. Task assignment situations were always central places of focus where employees interacted with the company and developed their work careers under lifetime employment.

Chapter 2 explains the development of the general framework. The method of the exploration is presented in chapter 3. Chapter 4 describes the growth and change of the target company, Tokyo Electric Company, Ltd. These provide the general organizational situations in which integration between the individual and the organization exists. Chapters 5-7 chronicle the relationships and interactions as integration develops. These chapters deal, respectively, with the engineers' early, mid, and late stages of career development. Chapter 8 presents the conclusion of this exploratory research and discusses its implications for research and management practices.

2

The General Framework

In this chapter I explain the development of the general framework with which I explored lifetime employment relationships and interactions between the individual and the organization. Using the framework, I focused on patterns and factors of integration between the two parties and collected data about them. Before presenting the framework, however, we will review and discuss the literature and concepts which relate to the issue of integration.

Literature about Integration between the Individual and the Organization

The issue of integration between the individual and the organization is discussed often in organizational behavior literature, but there are relatively few conceptual or empirical studies dealing directly with the issue. Most studies focus either on conditions for the attainment of organizational objectives, such as organizational effectiveness, or on conditions leading toward individual objectives in the organization, such as need satisfaction. However, we can select some major studies that focus directly on the issue of integration as one of their primary research points. These studies include:

Barnard, C.I. 1938. *The Functions of the Executive.*
Argyris, C. 1964. *Integrating the Individual and the Organization.*
Barrett, J.H. 1970. *Individual Goals and Organizational Objectives: A Study of Integration Mechanisms.*
Lorsch, J.W., and Morse, J.J. 1974. *Organizations and Their Members: A Contingency Approach.*
Schein, E.H. 1978. *Career Dynamics: Matching Individual and Organizational Needs.*

While these five studies are all concerned with American organizations, it is important to review them and discuss the current state of theoretical development as it deals directly with the issue of integration between the individual and the organization. After considering the condition of lifetime employment and shifting interest away from American organizations, I will develop the general framework relevant to the Japanese companies.

Literature Review

Constructing a general theory of organization as a cooperative system, Barnard (1938) focuses one of his major studies on the issue of integration between the individual and the organization. He argues that the accomplishment of organizational objectives formulated by the executive depends on contributions of actions made by organization members (effectiveness of the cooperative system), and that the organization must provide individual members with adequate incentives which can sufficiently satisfy their motives to induce those activities (efficiency of the system). In other words, the organization and the individual are integrated when the individual engages in activities which can contribute specifically to the achievement of the organization's objectives and when he receives enough inducements, material or social, to satisfy his needs in return for these contributions. This is integration by exchange of inducements (incentives) and contributions (activities) between the individual and the organization.

Barnard's study of integration between the individual and the organization is too general for specific practical application and does not precisely discuss the structure and dynamics of human needs. Therefore, it is very difficult to identify an effective linkage between organizational incentives and individual needs. Also, his investigation does not fully account for the effects of properties of organizational structure, nature of business, environment, etc., on the exchange of inducements and contributions. But it should be noted that Barnard provided the first theoretical and comprehensive discussion of integration between the individual and the organization in the literature of organizational behavior.

It should also be noted that March and Simon (1958) elaborate on Barnard's theory of inducements and contributions. However, the purpose of their study is not to focus more specifically on the issue of integration between the individual and the organization, but to explain the processes through which individuals go in deciding whether to participate in or leave an organization.

Argyris (1964) approaches the issue of integration between the individual and the organization more specifically. He focuses on organizations designed around classical organization theory.[1] He asserts that this type of organization is unhealthy for human beings because it eliminates opportunities for them to experience psychological success. Argyris regards psychological success as the most important thing for human beings to produce psychological energy, which can contribute to an increase in organizational effectiveness. Therefore, if individuals in an organization are unable to experience psychological success, organizational effectiveness will decrease.

Argyris proposes a theoretical remedy for an unhealthy organization, or an integration of the organization and the individual, through redesigning the organization to provide more activities in which its individual members can experience psychological success. Argyris presents six standards for the redesigning process (fig. 1).

Figure 1. Standards for Redesigning the Organization

1. The whole of the organization should be controlled by interrelationships of all parts, not by a specific part.

2. Individuals should be aware of the organization as a pattern of parts, not as a plurality of parts.

3. Organizational objectives should be achieved in relation to the whole, not to the parts.

4. The organization should be able to influence internal activities (achieving its objectives, maintaining the internal system).

5. The organization should be able to influence externally oriented activities.

6. The organization should be able to take into account the past history, the present, and the anticipated future of the organization in defining its activities to achieve the objectives, maintain the internal system, and adapt to the environment.

Source: Adapted from Argyris (1964)

Argyris asserts that this ideal organization affords the individual the highest probability of experiencing psychological success and creates maximum psychological energy, which increases organizational effectiveness. Argyris discusses various possible and practical ways to redesign the classical type organization so that it comes closer to the human relations type.

Redesigning an organization closer to Argyris' standards leads to a departure from the pyramidal organization design based on classical organization theory. The ideal organization which meets the six standards completely would have such fundamental characteristics as: each individual has equal power and responsibility to influence the organization; leaders and subordinates share the control of the group; and individuals produce as much of the total product as possible. Obviously, these characteristics are very similar to the properties of human relations theory.[2]

There is empirical evidence that seems to limit the universality of Argyris' theory of integration between the individual and the organization. Lawrence and Lorsch's (1967) empirical research reveals that classical and human relations theories work respectively in organizations under low- and high-uncertain environmental conditions, but not under reversed conditions. Lorsch and Morse (reviewed later) empirically add that satisfied individuals with high performance records in organizations under low- and high-uncertain environmental conditions possess congruent personality characteristics with the properties of classical and human relations theories, respectively. Therefore, Argyris' theory of integration seems to work only for classical type organizations under high-uncertain environmental conditions and with individuals whose personalities are oriented toward human relations theory.

Argyris' assumption that experiencing psychological success is the most important human need is supported by the motivators-hygiene theory (Herzberg, 1966). This says that primary determinants of satisfaction are intrinsic rewards such as achievement and growth, and that those of dissatisfaction are lack of extrinsic rewards such as pay and supervisory practices. Psychological success is obviously a type of intrinsic reward which can produce great individual satisfaction. Therefore, Argyris' suggestion of providing more activities for experiencing psychological success is correct, but does not take environmental, organizational, and personal conditions into consideration.

Barrett (1970) empirically demonstrates the importance of integration between the individual and the organization to the benefit of both parties. Barrett defines the degree of integration as the range of the individual's activities which can achieve respective objectives simultaneously. He also conceptualizes three methods for the organization to use to widen this range or to increase the degree of integration. The first is the exchange of extrinsic rewards, such as pay, for individual contributions to the achievement of organizational objectives. The second is the socialization of the individual to contribute more toward organizational objectives. The third is the accommodation of the organization to provide activities that are intrinsically rewarding to the individual and, at the same time, lead to the achievement of organizational objectives. Each method is supposed to encompass a number of specific integration practices.

Barrett found that the degree of integration between the individual and the organization is significantly associated with the quality of organizational functioning and individual motivation and satisfaction. Also he discovered that accommodation and exchange are respectively the most and least effective methods to generate a high degree of integration, and that socialization tends to be used simultaneously with accommodation, although the former is less effective than the latter. Furthermore, his data showed a slight tendency for organizational and personal factors to influence effectiveness. Barrett concluded that accommodation is the best method of integration between the individual and the organization. Obviously, this supports Argyris' theory of integration with the limitation of its universality.

However, Barrett's conceptualization of the degree and the methods of integration between the individual and the organization is too general to apply practically. His survey based on his conceptual model successfully demonstrates the importance of integration on an abstract level. It does not generate enough information to explain precisely how the range of activities can be enlarged and how they contribute to the simultaneous attainment of respective objectives. Barrett's study is important, however, because it is one of the few that empirically demonstrates the importance of the investigation of integration between the individual and the organization.

Lorsch and Morse's (1974) study is another example of scarce empirical studies of integration between the individual and the organization. In this case, more precise conditions for integration are investigated. Extending the contingency theory of organizations (Lawrence and Lorsch, 1967) to include the variable of the individual, Lorsch and Morse develop a "fit" concept for the simultaneous attainment of organizational and individual objectives. The theorists assert that "fit" or congruency among the external and the internal environments of the organization and the individual can facilitate simultaneous attainment of respective objectives.

The data empirically provided by Lorsch and Morse confirmed their expectations. High performing organizations under the low- and high-uncertain environmental conditions had respectively congruent internal organization climates and members with individual personalities. Low performing organizations under each of the environmental conditions had neither congruent climates nor members with congruent personalities. Moreover, individuals in high performing organizations felt a stronger sense of competence (i.e., were intrinsically more satisfied) than in low performing ones. The theorists concluded that the three-way "fit" among external and internal environmental factors and individual personality provides activities that lead simultaneously to effective performance in the organization and intrinsic satisfaction for the individual.

This study strongly supports Barrett's conclusion in more specific terms. Accommodating the organization to make a "fit" among the three components is a very effective integration mechanism. The accommodation can be accomplished by selecting the individual as well as by designing the organization. Furthermore, as has been explained earlier in this section, Lorsch and Morse's study implies that Argyris' theory of integration is applicable to a special case of misfit among the three components.

The "fit" condition is, however, static. It does not consider the dynamics of interaction between the individual and the organization. It is through these dynamics that objectives are achieved simultaneously. Moreover, the "fit" condition does not consider effects of this interaction, particularly on the individual's personality. Lorsch and Morse focus only on the relatively stable aspects of personality. Recent studies on the development of adult personality (Levinson, 1978, for example) present evidence that interaction with an organization is one important factor which causes the individual's personality to change.

Schein (1978) approaches the issue of integration between the individual and the organization by focusing on one of the dynamic aspects of their relationships—career development. This perspective differentiates Schein's study from the other four.

Schein explains that the individual has career-developmental needs generated by three different life cycles: the biological and social aging processes; the developmental relationships with the individual's family; and the occupational career cycle which is influenced mostly by an organization's policies for its employees. These life cycles interact and create roughly three stages of career development: early (entry to age 30), mid (age 25-45), and late (age 40 to retirement). Each of these stages presents problematic career issues (fig. 2). Overlapping periods among the three stages (age 25-30 and 40-45) show transitions into the next stages. The individual sees and experiences these stages and issues usually when he moves in organizational settings. Schein conceptually identifies three basic career moves: promotion, rotation, and permanent membership.

Figure 2. Career Issues

Early-career issues (entry-age 30)
1. Locating one's area of contribution
2. Learning how to fit into the organization
3. Becoming productive
4. Seeing a viable future for oneself in the career

Mid-career issues (age 25-45)
1. Locating one's career anchor and building one's career around it
2. Specializing versus generalizing

Late-career issues (age 40-retirement)
1. Becoming a mentor
2. Using one's experience and wisdom
3. Letting go and retiring

Source: Adapted from Schein (1978)

The individual needs to learn how to cope successfully with the issues in each career stage as he passes through it. At the same time, the organization also needs to effectively utilize its human resources to achieve its own objectives.

In order to match these needs of the two parties, Schein proposes a human resource planning and development system. In that system, Schein links human resource planning for staffing, development, leveling off, and replacement with career choice and the three stages of career development. The linkage is human resource management activities such as recruitment, training, job placement, performance appraisal, rotation, compensation, job design, etc. These activities must take into account the needs of the organization as well as the individual. For this purpose, Schein emphasizes the importance of job analysis on the side of the organization and assessment of career needs on the individual. It is these two analyses that provide necessary information to create an optimal match between the needs.

In particular, Schein suggests that human resource management activities should provide both optimally challenging job opportunities and accurate feedback on individual performance. He considers these two factors to be foundations for the growth and development of the individual and successful transitions into each new career stage.

Schein highlights human resource management activities for the generation of integration between the individual and the organization. These activities surround the job and contribute indirectly to the satisfaction of human needs and to the achievement of organizational objectives. Results of human resource management activities help the individual perform his job effectively. This effectiveness facilitates his coping with career issues and simultaneously contributes toward organizational effectiveness in the utilization of human resources to achieve the organization's objectives.

Schein's theory of integration between the individual and the organization is prescriptive. He presents general stages and issues of the life cycles and proposes important components of a human resource planning and development system. The theory works as a type of checklist for designing the system. However, it is difficult to use the theory conceptually to understand in what manner human resource management activities link the needs of the organization with those of the individual. The theory does not elaborate on how simultaneous satisfaction of these needs is achieved. Particularly, it does not conceptually explain why challenge and feedback are important to the simultaneous attainment of the objectives of the two parties.

Present Research Status

We have reviewed five studies which focused directly on the issue of integration between the individual and the organization. Although this number is small, these are the major and fundamental studies of integration in the area of organizational behavior. They are also conceptual or empirical studies. I believe it is possible and worthwhile to draw some conclusions from this review and to discuss its implications for the development of the general framework for our exploratory research.

Figure 3 is a comparison of the five studies. One of its essential points is that each study deals with integration between the individual and the organization as a relationship of exchange. Generally, when the individual's activities contribute toward the organization's objectives with mutual satisfaction, the two parties are integrated. In this context, Barnard's discussion on the exchange of inducements and contributions gives general insight into the issue of integration between the individual and the organization. Using this general model, each theorist proposes an integration mechanism for exchange with varying types of inducements and contributions to attain the two parties' objectives simultaneously.

Figure 3.   A Comparison of Five Studies of Integration
between the Individual and the Organization

	Barnard (1938)	Argyris (1964)	Barrett (1970)	Lorsch and Morse (1974)	Schein (1978)
Type of Study	Conceptual	Conceptual	Empirical	Empirical	Conceptual
Type of Individual	General	General	Manager, Worker	Manager	Manager
Type of Organization	General	Classical-theory-type	Business	Business	Business
Core Integration Mechanism	Exchange	Organization Redesign	1. Exchange 2. Socialization 3. Accommodation	Fit	Human Resource Planning and Development
What the Individual Receives	Inducements	Psychological Success	1. Extrinsic Rewards 2. None 3. Intrinsic Rewards	Sense of Competence	Satisfaction of Career-Developmental Needs
What the Organization Receives	Contributions	Psychological Energy	1. Necessary Activities 2. (same) 3. (same)	Effective Job Performance	Effective Utilization of Human Resources

The use of intrinsic rewards as inducements for the effective performance of job activities is a common suggestion in studies by Argyris, Barrett, and Lorsch and Morse. If the individual can expect such rewards from the activity itself, he will be highly motivated. The theorists propose that providing such kinds of activities is the most effective way to generate a high level of integration between the individual and the organization. Particularly, Lorsch and Morse's empirical study clearly reveals that a fit among external environment, internal environment, and individual is a crucial condition to generate these intrinsically motivating activities.

These three studies focus, implicitly or explicitly, on job activities. The organization expects effective job performance as a direct result of intrinsically rewarding job activities, and the individual receives such rewards in return for his effective performance. Schein's study differs in that it focuses on activities surrounding the job, that is, human resource management activities. Engaging in these activities helps the individual do a job better. This leads to individual career development and, simultaneously, the effective utilization of a human resource, thereby contributing indirectly toward the achievement of both the organization's and the individual's objectives. Schein's study deals with the context of integration between the individual and the organization (exchanges in activities surrounding the job), while the other three studies deal with the content of integration (exchanges in job activities). The literature review suggests that both types of activities are important factors to integration.

The socialization method of integration between the individual and the organization included in the study by Barrett has no relationship with exchange. Barrett finds that this method is second only to the accommodation method in effectiveness, and that it tends to be used simultaneously with the accommodation method. These findings seem to imply that a certain amount of socialization is a prerequisite to facilitating the accommodation method. Because the exchange of intrinsic rewards and job performance is intangible, and because the process of reaching an agreement about the exchange is not simple, the individual is required to carefully follow the implicit or explicit rules of the exchange. Socialization is an effective way for the individual to learn the rules quickly. The individual participates in socializing activities because he consciously or subconsciously understands these functions of the activities. This understanding of socialization is supported by Schein. He treats it as one of the important matching processes in the early period of an individual's career in the organization. Socialization helps the individual perform better in the organization.

From the literature review, I derived two fundamental implications for the development of a framework of integration between the individual and the organization under the conditions of lifetime employment. The first is that a simultaneous focus on both job activities and activities surrounding the job should be made. These two types of activities facilitate two different, but related, exchanges between the individual and the organization, that is, the content and context of integration.

This dichotomy is quite similar to Herzberg's (1966) motivation-hygiene theory.[3] Making an analogy to this theory, one could say that integration between the individual and the organization through job activities directly provides the simultaneous achievement of the individual's and the organization's objectives, and that additional integration through activities surrounding the job protects both parties from becoming incapable of achieving their objectives.

The essence of the Herzberg theory does not imply sole importance on the part of motivators. Instead, it asserts that motivators and hygiene factors complement each other. Hygiene factors create more effective contexts for motivators to encourage the individual to perform better. Similarly, integration between the individual and the organization through activities surrounding the job, particularly through human resource management activities, can present better contexts for integration through job activities. The individual who copes more easily with career issues can exchange more effective job performance with more intrinsic rewards. In order to take into account and examine this complementary relationship between the two types of integration, it is necessary to focus simultaneously on the two types of activities.

However, Herzberg's assumption that the same motivators and hygiene factors can motivate all people is too simple. In reality, different conditions motivate different people. Lorsch and Morse have already considered the effects of environmental, organizational, and personal differences on integration.

The second implication is that the dynamics of relationships between the individual and the organization should be considered. Except for Schein, the other researchers do not pay attention to the dynamic realities of the two parties: the individual changes because of changes in physiological, psychological, and social factors, and the organization changes under changing demands from external and internal conditions. Therefore, relationships between the two parties are inherently dynamic.

Schein deals with the dynamics of career development on the part of the individual. He examines its implications for activities surrounding the job, particularly human resource management activities. The rest assume static situations in the organization and the individual.

Another dynamic relevant to job activities is employee mobility in the organization. Individual skills and abilities develop and change as a result of job experiences or other activities. Also, changing demands from external and internal factors create a variety of jobs in the organization. These two kinds of changes generate hierarchical and vertical mobilities for individuals in the organization to establish job-to-person fits for effective performance. It is necessary to consider these dynamic mobilities in conjunction with the dynamics of career development.

Formation of the General Framework

The balance of this chapter develops the general framework, taking into account conclusions and implications made in the literature review. A conceptual linkage between Lorsch and Morse's study of integration between the individual and the organization through job activities and Schein's study of integration through activities surrounding the job is presented first. Based on that linkage, I combine the theorists' two conceptual frameworks to build my own, which guides the exploration of integration between the individual and the organization under the conditions of lifetime employment. The conceptual linkage will rationalize my framework.

The studies of Lorsch and Morse and Schein are chosen because they are the latest and the most comprehensive among the five major studies reviewed. Lorsch and Morse effectively use a contingency approach to focus on patterns and relationships among a variety of variables related to integration between the individual and the organization. Schein uses a career development perspective on the dynamic interaction between the two parties.

It is important to note that these studies, based on American organizations, do not entirely fit the conditions of Japanese lifetime employment under which the general framework is developed. For example, Lorsch and Morse do not take into account that the personality of the individual changes as a result of interaction with the organization. In American organizations, where the individual often pursues a multi-organization career during a lifetime, personality change may not be an important consideration to generate integration between the individual and the organization; under single-organization, lifetime employment, it is a crucial factor.

Schein emphasizes the importance of the discovery and development of the individual's "career anchor" (which is discussed later) in passing from the early to mid stages of a multi-organization career. The career anchor helps the individual decide what he should do in his total life, and it places a direction on the process of moving from and to organizations to find the most suitable one. However, when the individual pursues a single-organization career under lifetime employment, he may develop less need for a career anchor because he needs only to identify what he can do in the given organization.

Schein also discusses the importance of tenure at the mid-career stage. After the individual receives tenure from an organization, implicitly or explicitly, he is expected to contribute more than he learns. In the Japanese lifetime employment system, which grants tenure immediately, learning and contributing by the individual may be given equal emphasis.

To begin conceptually linking integration between the individual and the organization through job activities and activities surrounding the job, Schein's conceptual model is examined first. Schein investigates various components of a human resource planning and development system to help individual members of an organization develop their careers and, at the same time, perform effectively. Schein asserts that this human resource management system should provide performance evaluation feedback and optimally challenging job opportunities.

There are three studies which conceptually supplement Schein's theory. White (1963) states that man's most fundamental need is to use his own competencies to influence and master his external environment. When this is accomplished, he feels a sense of competence, which is a kind of intrinsic reward, and becomes satisfied that he has adequate and sufficient capacity to interact effectively with his environment. White emphasizes the importance of performance evaluation feedback to enhance this feeling of intrinsic satisfaction. The feedback tells the individual how effectively he deals with the requirements of the environment.

Deci (1975) argues that when the difficulty of a task is optimally challenging to one's existing abilities, he will conquer the challenge, thereby increasing his abilities and performing more effectively. However, if the challenge is too great or too small, he will not be motivated or satisfied and will feel that the task is not suitable for his abilities.

Hall (1971) sees career development as a process of increasing one's sense of self-esteem by seeking task situations where his self-esteem will be enhanced and avoiding task situations where it will be reduced. Hall argues that one feels an increased sense of self-esteem when he uses his competencies to deal successfully with an optimally challenging task assignment and experiences psychological success. As a result, he becomes further motivated and committed to tackle his next task assignment. From this evolves an ever continuing career development cycle of performing a challenging task assignment, experiencing psychological success, and increasing self-esteem and motivation.

Based on these three supplementary studies, I interpret Schein's conceptual position as: when the individual successfully completes a task assignment which is optimally challenging to his existing abilities, he receives intrinsic rewards, such as a psychological feeling of success and a sense of competence and self-esteem. Task accomplishment means effective job performance to the organization. Performance evaluation feedback tells the individual how much effect he has on the organization or the environment, and it contributes toward his feeling of satisfaction and motivation to perform the next task assignment more effectively.

This interpretation emphasizes that it is a basic function of human resource management activities to put the individual in the intrinsic, self-reinforcing motivation process. Receiving optimally challenging job opportunities and performance evaluation feedback, the individual goes successfully through the cycle of task accomplishment, intrinsic satisfaction, and motivation toward the next task assignment. His growth and career development are promoted by repeating this process continuously.

The style of this interpretation is similar to that of recent studies of job design (especially Hackman and Lawler, 1971, and Hackman and Oldham, 1976) which demonstrate the importance of meaningful job characteristics (e.g., variety, wholeness of work, autonomy) and performance feedback to the intrinsic motivation and satisfaction of workers. However, this approach is based on a different assumption from Schein's concept of intrinsic motivation. The theorists assume that all individuals have a need for self-actualization. When an individual with this need accomplishes a job which has meaningful characteristics and for which he receives evaluation feedback, he becomes intrinsically satisfied. On the other hand, our interpretation of Schein's study assumes a need to use one's own existing abilities to interact effectively with his environment. This assumption precludes the necessity to agree that all individuals must realize the same inherent potentialities. We can accept, however, that individuals have different levels and types of abilities.

It should be noted that Schein uses the concept of "career anchor" to describe the individual's career in the perspective of his total life. The individual's career anchor is a basic combination of self-perceived abilities, needs, and values which have emerged gradually through interactions with his family, education, and work-related environments. The career anchor stabilizes the direction of his career decisions such as those to move from one company to another. He recognizes, based on his career anchor, what he is good at, and that it coincides with what he values in his total life.

If Schein's discussion of the career anchor is confined to that part of one's life space in which he interacts with his employing organizations, then the essential component of his career anchor becomes his competencies and characteristics relevant to task assignments in the organizations. This component guides and constrains the individual to seek challenging task assignments in one organization after another.

Under the condition of lifetime employment, that process does not happen interorganizationally, but intraorganizationally. This facilitates our exploratory study of integration between the individual and the organization, since we need only to focus entirely on the interacting area of the individual's life space within his given organization. This area occupies the main part of his total life space because of the conditions of lifetime employment.

Lorsch and Morse's conceptual position is now examined to determine a linkage with Schein's model. The essence of Lorsch and Morse's theory is that the three-way fit among external environment, internal environment, and individual personality promotes the individual's effective job performance in the organization and facilitates his intrinsic satisfaction in job accomplishment simultaneously.

To explain this requirement of fit, Lorsch and Morse take an information processing view of organization and individual. The organization's external environment consists of a body of information which the organization uses to achieve its objectives. These objectives are accomplished by the organization's individual members through information gathering, information transmission, and decision making. The individual uses his own information processing capacity, which includes competencies and characteristics relevant to the task, in the manner of performance which he perceives is expected by the organization. His expectations stem from the internal environment which is composed of a set of signals shaped by formal organizational rules and practices, and by expectations of supervisors, subordinates, and peers.

An optimum fit among external and internal environments and individual personality is found through the best possible combination of the type of information, the expected way to process this information, and the individual's information processing capacity. This situation becomes the task assignment situation for the individual, in which the fit allows him to use his abilities most effectively to accomplish the task. The individual feels an increased sense of competence in the successful completion of the task and becomes intrinsically satisfied and motivated to perform the next task assignment.

From the discussion so far, it has become clear that "intrinsic motivation" is the conceptual linkage between Lorsch and Morse's study of integration between the individual and the organization through job activities and Schein's study of integration through activities surrounding the job. Individuals are intrinsically motivated to perform their jobs when they expect intrinsic rewards, such as a psychological feeling of success and a sense of competence and self-esteem, in the completion of the jobs. They are encouraged even when the only reward is the accomplishment of the activity itself.

Lorsch and Morse's study asserts that the individual is motivated when he performs a job in the task situation which congruently combines the type of information from the external environment, the way of processing information furnished by the organization's structure and processes, and his competencies to process the information. The individual can accomplish the job successfully in that task situation. Schein's study complementarily explains that the organization's human resource management, which provides optimal challenge and performance evaluation feedback for the individual, facilitates his feeling of intrinsic satisfaction in the completion of the job and motivation toward the next one. The individual's career development is promoted by repeating such an intrinsically motivating task assignment.

The General Framework

This final section of the chapter presents my general framework based on the previous discussion of the linkage between Lorsch and Morse's and Schein's studies. The linkage suggests that Schein's framework which focuses on activities surrounding the job conceptually complements Lorsch and Morse's framework which focuses on job activities.

Figure 4 shows my general framework, which is a combination of the two previously explained frameworks. Its essential feature is that the individual's career path under lifetime employment is conceptually understood as a sequence of task assignments in the organization. The individual performs a variety of task assignments, one after another, from the time of entry through retirement. In the figure the assignments are numbered sequentially from 1 through n for convenience. Going through this sequence, the individual develops his own career which consists of early, mid, and late stages and the transitions among them.

The sequence also implies horizontal or vertical mobility by the individual in the organization. Sometimes he is assigned (transferred) to a task in a differently functioning department in the organization, but maintains the same level of responsibility. Or he may be assigned (promoted) to a more responsible task and receive a higher position in the organization's hierarchy.

Each assignment places the individual in a task assignment situation where he accomplishes the task. A rectangle divided into four triangles in the lower part of the figure schematically represents a task assignment situation. The nature of the situation varies from assignment to assignment. Its determinant is based upon the four factors indicated in the triangles: external environment; individual; organizational climate for job performance; and organizational climate for growth and development.

The "external environment" consists of information about market, technological, scientific, economic, and social factors relevant to the task the individual performs to achieve the organization's goals. Because a manufacturing organization is the focus of this exploratory study, environments are related to manufacturing, marketing, or research and development. Although the source of particular information may be physically located in the organization (e.g., production technology, scientific experiments, market research data), this author conceives of it as constituting the external environment since the information is the material with which the individual deals to make decisions.

The "individual" accomplishes the task using his relevant competencies

Figure 4. The General Framework

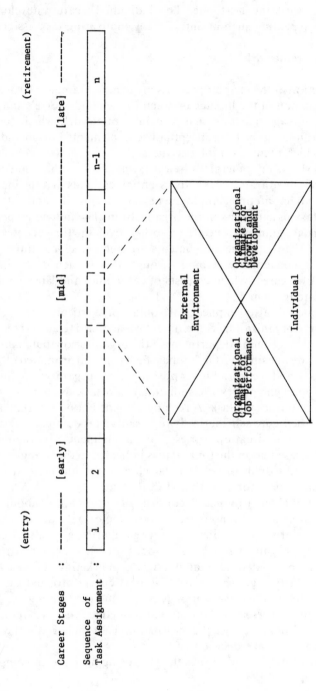

Career Stages : —— [early] —————— [mid] ———————— [late] ———

(entry)   (retirement)

Sequence of
Task Assignment :

| 1 | 2 | | n-1 | n |

External
Environment

Organizational
Climate for
Growth and
Development

Organizational
Climate for
Job Performance

Individual

Task Assignment Situation

and characteristics. These are skills and knowledge accumulated in past education and job experiences, and his innate personality traits. These abilities may increase or somehow change as a result of the task accomplishment. He receives intrinsic rewards from accomplishing the task, and feels satisfied and motivated toward tackling the next task assignment.

The "organizational climate for job performance" provides the individual with work settings that regulate his method of performing the job. The climate is generated by the formal organizational and measurement practices and by expectations of people around the individual. He learns explicitly and implicitly from this climate how to relate to the work of the organization in dealing with the external environment. (Lorsch and Morse labeled this concept of the climate as "internal environment.")

Information and opportunities that help the individual grow and develop his career create the "organizational climate for growth and development." Particularly, the organization's human resource management, which involves the individual in such activities as training, placement, performance appraisal, rotation, promotion, compensation, and so on, plays an important role in generating the climate. Participating in those activities, the individual learns how effectively he performs the job and how much impact he makes on the organization or the environment. Also, he receives opportunities to use his competencies to deal effectively with the external environment. Through these opportunities and information, the individual perceives the organizational climate helping him grow and develop his career.

The purpose of the general framework is to guide the exploration of lifetime employment relationships and interactions between the individual and the organization. The idea of intrinsic motivation which conceptually links the two types of integration between the individual and the organization helps "form" the framework. Hypothesis testing, if the linkage is empirically true, is not the aim of this research; describing the phenomena is. The linkage is expected to suggest that the general framework is available as a conceptual convenience.

In fact, the framework will serve as a "map" for the exploration. With this, we can describe and examine task assignment situations where the individual is, or is not, intrinsically motivated and better understand the process of the individual's career development and integration with the organization under the conditions of lifetime employment.

3

Methodology

Exploration

The purpose of the research is to explore the lifetime employment relationships and interactions between the individual and the organization. This chapter explains the design and process of this exploration.

The target company for the exploration is Tokyo Electric Co., Ltd. established in the 1930s. It employed about 13,000 people in 1982. The company's products are electric materials, parts, devices and instruments, and systems made up of those components.

This particular research site was selected because the company manufactures and sells its products almost entirely in Japan, and its management is typically Japanese. The founder of the company is one of the Japanese entrepreneurs who established the so-called "Japanese management system" in their enterprises. The success of this management system and the high productivity of the parent corporation and its group companies, one of which is Tokyo Electric, are highly publicized.

The general framework developed in chapter 2 proposes some important areas for focus. Particularly, the framework suggests that each individual's task assignment situation can be viewed through four considerations: external environment; the individual; organizational climate for job performance; and organizational climate for growth and development. The framework also suggests that the individual goes through the early, mid, and late stages of career development while continuously performing task assignments. The design of data collection must be made based on these suggestions.

A longitudinal research method that traces and examines the individual's task assignments would seem initially to be most appropriate. But it is obviously impossible since it would take too long to track the career development of a group of subjects over approximately 40 years from recruitment to retirement.

The Japanese practice of lifetime employment, however, affords a unique opportunity to use a "quasi-longitudinal" approach, namely, to collect historical data. I explored all task assignment situations, from career entry to the present, of the 27 engineers who were the research subjects. They had all started their work careers in Tokyo Electric immediately after graduation, and had continued to develop their careers by performing task assignments in the company.

Design

Twenty-seven engineers with university backgrounds were selected as subjects in Tokyo Electric Company, Ltd. They were between 44 and 49 years old at the time of the research in 1982. The logic of using this specific age bracket is derived from Levinson's (1978) findings that individuals experience transitions from early to mid stages of career development during the age period of 28-33 and transitions from mid to late stages during the age period of 40-45.[1] In order to arrive at the 44-49 year age bracket, 4 years were added to each end of the transition period from mid to late stages. By doing this, it was intended to include the subjects who had already experienced the early and the mid stages of career development and were now at the late stage.

There is another important dimension that created the configuration of the 27 subjects. They were almost evenly selected from three different organizational units: the Research and Development Laboratory (8 subjects), the Lighting Division Group (10 subjects), and the Small Appliances Division Group (9 subjects). While some had experienced their first few task assignments in other units before being transferred to their present unit, most of the subjects had been assigned tasks in the same organizational unit since their entry to the company.

The purpose of selecting subjects from the three organizational units was to take account of task assignments in research, manufacturing, and marketing. The subjects in the Research and Development Laboratory (R&D Lab) had performed research and development task assignments; those in the Lighting Division Group had performed tasks mainly in product planning and development, sales engineering, and quality examination; and the engineers in the Small Appliances Division Group had performed tasks in manufacturing or product planning and development.

The decision to include task assignments from all the three basic areas of manufacturing-business operations was based on knowledge of studies made by Lawrence and Lorsch (1967) and Lorsch and Morse (1974). The theorists found that these tasks are performed in organizational segments which have different organizational structures and processes, and that individuals performing the tasks tend to have different personality characteristics.

The final criterion used in selecting the subjects was that they had experienced at least two major promotions in their career development with the company: promotions to the section manager level (the middle-management level) and to the department manager level (the upper middle-management level). In fact, 24 of the 27 subjects had positions at the department manager level in 1982. Three of them had been further promoted to assistant division general manager in 1981, and one of the three attained the position of division general manager in 1982.

Process

Access to the data sources was requested through a letter to a top manager of the Department of Human Resource Management (HRM) in Tokyo Electric Co., Ltd. When the access was granted in May 1982, I met with the top manager and a section manager in the department to explain the purpose and method of the research. The HRM department handles all transfers and promotions of headquarters-based employees in the company.

The author met with the section manager and some of his staff a few times. Details of the data collection process were discussed and the research subjects were selected. The HRM department announced formally to the laboratory and the two division groups that the department was cooperating in the collection of data for a research study and requested their cooperation.

During the meetings, written information about the organization and its human resource management systems was requested. The information typically took the form of organization charts, a corporate history published by the company, manuals of the HRM systems, sample forms used in the systems, past company newspapers distributed by the department to all employees, annual reports, and recruitment booklets. Information about the systems in action and their historical development was also requested.

Early in June, meetings were scheduled with three high-ranking managers from the R&D Lab, the Lighting Division Group, and the Small Appliances Division Group. They were interviewed individually for about one and one-half hours. At each meeting, the purpose and method of the research was explained, and then questions about the business, organizational structure, essential tasks, and historical development and background of the organization unit were asked. An interview guide was used for asking questions (see app. A). Written materials, such as unit organization charts and product brochures, were also requested.

After these meetings, the HRM department, in cooperation with the three organizational units, began scheduling individual interviews with the 27 research subjects. The department requested supervisors of the subjects to release them for these interview meetings.

While the scheduling was being arranged, the author learned more about the company and its organization. The written materials received from the

HRM department and the three organization units were checked. The interview notes taken in the meetings with the HRM section manager and his staff and the three unit managers were also carefully reviewed.

The individual interviews were conducted through late June to early October in 1982. Each interview was two to three hours long. Approximately two-thirds of the interviews were held at the company headquarters, and the rest at other areas where the subjects were located. All interviews were done during work time.

A friendly atmosphere in the interview room was created to ensure cooperation and freedom of expression. For this purpose, a Japanese "tatami room" was used for the interview. Tatami is a straw matting used as a floor covering in a typical Japanese home. Although the company's offices were not of that type, such rooms were available at all interview locations for employees' social or recreational use.

It is customary for a Japanese person to feel relaxed when he takes off his shoes at the entrance of a tatami home and sits on a cushion on the tatami floor. By re-creating this atmosphere, the author hoped to achieve a homey effect.

At each meeting, the interviewer welcomed the interview subject at the doorway to the tatami room. The subject took off his shoes, walked into the room, and sat on the cushion on the tatami floor. The first five to ten minutes were spent in casual conversation explaining briefly the background and purpose of the research. The interviewer emphasized the purely academic purpose for the study and answered the subject's questions about it before starting the interview itself. Coffee or tea was served in the privacy of the interview room.

The purpose of the introductory period of the meeting was to help relax the subject and free his mind from his work. After this initial period, questions about the subject's task assignment situations were asked using an interview guide (see app. B).

The interview typically followed several steps. First, the interviewer asked the subject to identify turning points in his career development with the company. Usually these were transfers, promotions, or other movements caused by organizational changes. The subject was told to consider only movement which created a substantial change in jobs as a turning point. Second, the subject was asked to describe briefly all task assignments since his entry to the company through the time of the interview. Then, the interviewer asked in detail about each task assignment situation, focusing roughly on the four aspects identified in the general framework of this exploratory study; he also asked about the transition to each task assignment.

It is important to note that the interview session was not a question-and-answer period. The interviewer firmly kept the role of "listener" during the

Figure 5.　Information and Its Sources

INFORMATION	SOURCE				
	Interviews with the Subject	Interviews with the Managers of the Org. Units	Interviews with the HRM Managers	Printed Materials	Personnel Files
Development of the Organization	*	**	*	**	*
Sequence of the Individual's Task Assignments	**				**
Task Assignment Situation:					
Jobs	**	*		*	*
Competencies	**				**
Climate for Performance	**	**		**	*
Climate for Growth and Development	**	*	**	**	
Results	**				**
Transition to the Next Assignment	**			*	*

**—a main source; *—a supplementary source

interview, asking questions simply to evoke the subject's story of each task assignment situation and to keep him on the track. Twenty to 30 pages of notes were taken during each interview. A tape recorder was not used because of the possibility of making the subjects nervous.

After each day's interviews, data from the personnel files of the day's subjects were collected from the HRM department. With the assistance of HRM staff, information about the subjects' records of transfers, promotions, performance appraisals, and supervisors' comments was recorded. When the interview location was not near the headquarters area, these personnel data were collected on the next earliest possible day. On the night of an interview, the interviewer carefully reviewed his interview notes to correct errors and fill in blank spaces.

All interviews were repeated in the same manner described above. In late October the interviewer had the final meeting with the top manager and the section manager in the HRM department. He asked them to clarify information about the organization which he had either encountered in the interview or found in reviewing his notes.

Overview

Enormous amounts of information concerning the organization and the individuals were collected as a result of the exploration. There were several areas into which the information was categorized: data on the development of the organization; information about the sequence of the individual's task assignments; and information on each task assignment situation of the individual, covering the individual's jobs (the external environment), competencies, organizational climates for job performance and growth and development, results in the assignment (performances and feelings), and transition to the next assignment. Figure 5 shows the relationship of sources to the categorized information. Because the information came from multiple data sources, its validity could be examined.

4

The Company

This chapter reviews briefly the economic growth of Tokyo Electric Company, Ltd., during the quarter-century study period from 1957 to 1982 and describes its major organizational characteristics.[1] As will be shown, the fundamental structure of the organization and the basic process of human resource management based on lifetime employment were fairly constant during this period.

The Quarter-Century Study Period: 1957-82

Figures 6 and 7 demonstrate the remarkable growth and development of the Japanese economy and, specifically, Tokyo Electric during the quarter-century study period. Japan's nominal Gross National Product (GNP) increased from 11 trillion yen in 1957 to 260 trillion yen in 1982.

Although the nominal GNP steadily increased, the real growth rate of the economy showed two different phases—before and after the 1973 oil crisis. There was a great spurt of economic growth prior to the crisis in which the average real growth rate of the economy reached 10%. However, a slower average growth rate of only 3.7% marked the period from 1973 to 1982.

The growth of sales at Tokyo Electric was remarkable during the quarter-century study period, too. Its sales of about 500 billion yen in 1982 were 79 times larger than the 1957 figure of 6.3 billion yen.

It is indicated in the research that Tokyo Electric's growth was largely the result of a constantly high dependency on the Japanese market during the quarter-century study period. The company exported only 3.0% of its total products in 1960, 2.4% in 1970, 4.2% in 1980, and 4.7% in 1982. This constantly high dependency was probably due to the company's focusing on fundamentally the same electric product categories, most of which were related to the construction of buildings and houses.

However, the company experienced two major profit decreases, one in 1975 and the other in 1982, affected by domestic economic recessions. Their

Figure 6.   Nominal GNP and Real Growth Rate in Japan

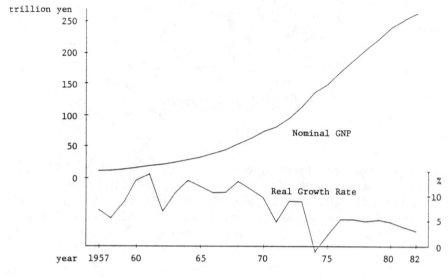

Source: *Handbook of the Economy*, Economic Planning Agency, 1983

Figure 7.   Sales and Profit before Taxes at Tokyo Electric Company, Ltd.

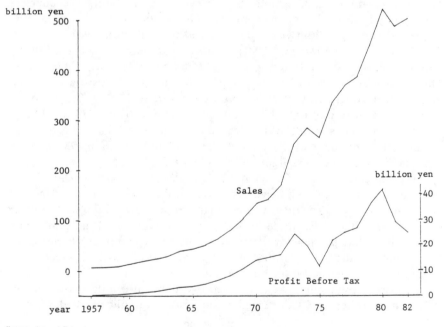

Source: Annual Reports

The Company 31

small amount of exports could not hedge their domestic sales slumps. The construction rates for buildings and houses were sensitive to the nation's economy, but as is seen in the following sections, these profit drops hardly affected the fundamental characteristics of the organization.

Organizational Structure

Tokyo Electric's organizational structure remained essentially the same during the quarter-century study period. It consisted of three organizational segments: headquarters, manufacturing, and marketing. The headquarters segment consisted of administrative departments and central laboratories, one of which was the Research and Development Laboratory concerned in this research. The manufacturing segment was composed of product divisions. These included the Lighting Division and the Small Appliances Division, which in 1971 grew into the division groups. The marketing segment had area sales divisions.[2]

Product and area sales divisions operated as independent profit centers. Relationships between them were "matrix": products from each product division were sold directly to area sales divisions whose local sales offices sold to users through wholesalers in their areas.

Each product division was subdivided into product or functional departments. Departments were further subdivided into sections. Area sales divisions were composed of sales offices, which were organizationally at the same level as division departments. Sales offices were also subdivided into sections. However, administrative departments and laboratories of the headquarters segment were subdivided only into headquarters sections such as laboratory sections (organizationally at the same level as division departments and sales offices).

Originally, there were 10 product divisions in the manufacturing segment. Each division dealt with several related product lines. In some cases, more than one division dealt with similar product lines. When a set of product lines in a division grew large enough to become independent, the company created a new product division usually by separating from the parent division. The number of product divisions increased to 16 in 1971.

Conflicts among divisions in product development and manufacturing were intensified as the number of divisions grew. To cope with the problem of competition among divisions with similar product lines, the company introduced a division group structure in 1971. Group executives, who were at director level or above, were appointed to coordinate the divisions.

The Lighting Division Group and the Small Appliances Division Group were formed in 1971. Their component divisions, which included lighting and small appliances, had existed prior to this formation. Until 1982, there was no fundamental change in the group structure of the organization, although the company had added or deleted some product divisions.

Human Resources

The recruitment policy of Tokyo Electric remained the same during the quarter-century study period. Staffing of the organization was obtained almost entirely through the employment of new graduates from universities, high schools, or junior highs. Because graduation was in March in Japan, the company engaged in periodic recruitment every April.[3]

The number of entrants who were not new graduates was in fact very small. For example, only about 1% of headquarters-based employees were, at the time of the research, mid-career or lateral entrants. Furthermore, an average of about 1% of the headquarters-based employees annually resigned in the first 10 years after recruitment. Resignation after the 10-year mark was very rare.

Every new graduate entering the company was assigned to one of three relatively broad areas of career specialization based on educational background and company needs. The areas of specialization were: manual labor; technological career areas for product development and engineering; and nonproduction career areas for administrative staff services and marketing. Switching from one career area to another was relatively rare. All of the engineers in this research study were in the technological career areas.

Manual workers for manufacturing were hired locally at each factory. The company tended to employ people with junior high or high school educations for this career area.

On the other hand, the company recruited candidates with university, or at least high school, educations for the technological and nonproduction career areas. Usually, those with scientific or engineering backgrounds entered the technological career areas. They were placed mostly in laboratories or product divisions. Those with backgrounds in languages, literature, commerce, economics, and law entered the nonproduction career areas. They were assigned to staff service jobs in headquarters departments or to marketing jobs in sales divisions. Sometimes, they had administrative jobs in product divisions.

All employees of Tokyo Electric were expected to be loyal and to stay for a lifetime, that is, from recruitment right after graduation through retirement at the mandatory age. Retirement age was extended from 55 to 60 in the early 1970s. Because of this, the importance of sharing the company's philosophy was emphasized among all members.[4] This philosophy essentially presented the spirit of unity and mutual help among employees and the responsibility of the manufacturer to contribute toward society through production.

The Ranking System

Because virtually all members of Tokyo Electric had been employed right after graduation and remained loyal to the company, seniority was inevitably considered as an indicator of advancement in the organization. The maintenance of seniority consistency through recruitment, promotion, rotation, compensation, education, or other treatment of employees was the task of the headquarters HRM department. The company centralized these essential personnel functions in this department.[5] Particularly, the maintenance of seniority consistency was related heavily to an elaborate system of formal ranking, which was established and operated by the department.

This ranking system remained uniform throughout the study period.[6] Because all of the 27 engineers interviewed in the research were headquarters-based employees, we will focus on that part of the system related to the headquarters-based employees in the technological career areas.

Figure 8 shows the ranking system. One of the essential points of the figure is that nonmanagerial jobs under the supervision of section managers were graded into four hierarchical ranks: NMJ1, NMJ2, NMJ3, and NMJ4.[7] These ranks form the nonmanagerial level of the organization, and were applied uniformly to all jobs performed by nonmanagerial engineers in laboratories and product divisions. Therefore, an engineer performing a basic research job in the R&D Lab at the rank of NMJ3 was regarded as at the same status as an NMJ3 engineer who performed a product development job at a division.

Qualifications for these job rankings were determined by years of experience on the job, or seniority. Every new university graduate entered the company at the rank of NMJ1.[8] After two years of experience at NMJ1, he was promoted to NMJ2, and in three more years he became an NMJ3. Up to the NMJ3 rank, promotions were automatic.

In another three years, promotion from NMJ3 to NMJ4 was possible, based on merit as well as seniority. In principle, the highest performers of the same-seniority echelon were promoted in the year. A year later, the second highest performers were promoted, and the rest were promoted two years later. It was considered fairly standard to remain at the NMJ3 level for four years.

Promotion from the NMJ4 rank to the section manager level was based on the same principle, although the number of years served at this rank was more flexible.

This study indicated that experiencing the process of merit-based promotion caused employees of the same seniority to realize that the company identified fast, average, and slow runners in the echelon. However, this awareness of competition was only realized within the same-seniority echelon.

Figure 8.　The Ranking System

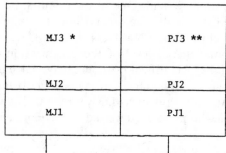

Chairman of the Board of Directors
President
Executive Vice President
Senior Managing Director
Managing Director
Director

Division General Manager

Assistant
Division General Manager

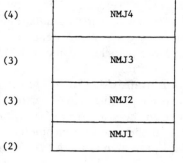

MJ3 *	PJ3 **	: The Department Manager Level
MJ2	PJ2	
MJ1	PJ1	: The Section Manager Level

(4) NMJ4

(3) NMJ3

(3) NMJ2   : The Non-Managerial Level

NMJ1
(2)

Minimum Years
to Stay for

*,** :　MJ3: Department Manager　　　　　　PJ3: Principal Professional
　　　　MJ2: Assistant Department Manager　PJ2: Associate Professional
　　　　MJ1: Section Manager　　　　　　　　PJ1: Assistant Professional

Job performances at all ranks except for NMJ1 were appraised based on job descriptions prepared by the HRM department. The department used relatively general terms in job descriptions because job ranks were fairly broadly defined. There were only four uniform ranks of nonmanagerial jobs performed by headquarters-based employees in laboratories and divisions, for example.

Although performances were appraised at all ranks above NMJ1, results were never formally fed back to employees. Furthermore, performance appraisals were considered in promotion decisions only beyond the NMJ3 rank. Therefore, employees had difficulty linking their evaluations to their actual job activities.

As a formal procedure, the HRM department requested supervisors to appraise the performance of each of their subordinates every December. This was done separately by the employee's direct supervisor and by the supervisor's supervisor.

Each of these two supervisors appraised the subordinate's performance using a two-part form. The first part was a general evaluation of job performance throughout one year, using a numerical scoring system. The second part was an evaluation of the employee's abilities, such as "knowledge in the job area," "analysis and planning abilities," "judgment," "human relation skills," and "personality." (These items were for the NMJ3 and NMJ4 ranks. Different items were used for other ranks.) A numerical score was obtained on this part also.

Then, each supervisor calculated a total performance appraisal score by adding the job performance score and the employee's ability score, giving the performance score 40%-50% weight on the total score. The supervisor was also required to comment on the employee's strengths and weaknesses and overall personality.

The department calculated an integrated performance appraisal score for each employee based on the two supervisors' total scores. This integrated score became the basic information for promotion and compensation of employees. The identification of fast, average, and slow runners in same-seniority echelons was based primarily on these scores.

Jobs above the rank of NMJ4 were managerial and professional. Managerial jobs were graded at MJ1, MJ2, and MJ3. These ranks were related directly to the job titles of section manager, assistant department manager, and department manager, respectively.

Professional jobs were graded PJ1, PJ2, and PJ3 and were related to the job titles of assistant professional, associate professional, and principal professional, respectively. These professionals were expected to perform in an advanced technological position and to supervise engineers below them. Professionals were not usually responsible for the management of their sections or departments. As indicated in figure 8, paired ranks of managerial and professional jobs were considered organizationally to have the same status.

It should be emphasized that the company placed only the people whose job capabilities were at the MJ rank in managerial positions. This is one of the most important points of the ranking system. The promotion of other people to the professional job ranks led to the reduction of demands for managerial positions. Furthermore, it contributed toward the promotion of the people who did not want a managerial job to higher positions in the organization.

Promotion to MJ1 or PJ1 ranks was considered after an employee completed at least four years at the NMJ4 rank. If his integrated performance appraisal scores in the latest three years met certain requirements and if his supervisor recommended him for promotion, he became a candidate for promotion. The HRM department then required him to take a part-time, six-month training program within the company, in which he wrote research papers and took psychological and managerial tests. During the program, staff of the HRM department interviewed each of the candidates. Promotion was then based on a comprehensive review of performance appraisals and the results of the training program and interviews. Selection for either managerial or professional ranks was made by the department.

In the promotion decision to MJ1 or PJ1 ranks, merit was considered, but only within the same-seniority echelon. As in the promotion process to NMJ3 and NMJ4, candidates who were identified in the comprehensive review as fast runners in the same-seniority group were promoted first, and seniority based on merit was maintained as much as possible.

The promotion procedure to MJ2 or PJ2 ranks was almost the same as that to MJ1 or PJ1. But in many cases in product divisions, a job at the MJ2 rank was regarded as training for a job at MJ3, and therefore an employee was often promoted to MJ2 in divisions when a position at the MJ3 level was anticipated in the future.

Promotion to MJ2 or PJ2 rank or above were much more competitive than to MJ1 or PJ1 at least within the same-seniority echelon. In fact, a tiny percentage were promoted after, let's say, five years at MJ1 or PJ1 rank. Most would have to wait at least some more years. Some employees reached the mandatory retirement age before promotion although many made it as far as MJ3 or PJ3 rank by retirement because of seniority. Promotion beyond this level was regarded as recognition of superior management achievement and capacity.

The major parts of individual monthly salaries and biannual bonuses were related directly to ranks. There were pay formulas defined for each rank. Using integrated performance appraisal scores, each formula provided annual salary increases for employees at each rank, and determined major portions of their bonuses paid in the year. When promotion to one rank higher was made, the formula of the higher rank was applied. This generated a substantial increase in salaries and bonuses.

While these financial benefits were linked to ranks, they increased according to seniority at least up to the NMJ4 rank because ranks below this were based completely on seniority. Furthermore, even beyond this level, they increased based fundamentally on seniority because merit-based promotion was made within the overriding emphasis on seniority.

During the quarter-century study period from 1957 through 1982, the overall organizational characteristics of Tokyo Electric Company, Ltd., remained fairly constant except for the increase in the size of organization and the amount of production and sales. This increase was achieved with no fundamental change in the divisionalized structure of the organization and with a consistently high emphasis on the same product categories and the domestic market. In order to facilitate the growth of manufacturing and sales, the company staffed its organization almost entirely through the employment of new graduates from universities, high schools, or junior highs. They were employed for a lifetime and treated uniformly by the company's human resource management system, which was an elaborate system of formal ranking based on merit with an overriding emphasis on seniority. The 27 engineers interviewed had developed their work careers in this lifetime employment situation in a typically Japanese company.

5

The Engineers at the Early-Career Stage: 1957-66

We will now examine the long-term relationships and interactions between the individual and the organization under the conditions of lifetime employment. This chapter examines the period from 1957 to 1966 when the 27 engineers interviewed for this study were at the early stage of their career development with Tokyo Electric Company. They spent this time performing various first-line, technological task assignments and learning about working under lifetime employment. The engineers had joined the company between 1957 and 1961, and their ages at entrance varied from 22 to 27, depending on years spent in universities. In 1966, they became 28-33 years old and were in the transition to the mid-career stage.[1]

Entrance

It can be said, based on my findings, that one of the most important aspects of human resource management based on the Japanese lifetime employment system is that new graduates are employed not to fill immediate, specific job slots but as a pool of resources to be shared in the organization and used as needed. The new recruit does not expect to acquire a specific job in the company but feels that he has taken on a lifetime commitment and loyalty to the company as a whole.

In Tokyo Electric, the HRM department managed headquarters-based employment. Every year the department forecast the company's headquarters-based work force needs based on manpower requests made by divisions. In the case of recruitment for the technological career areas, the department determined, based on manpower requests, how many new graduates would be needed in each technological area, such as electronics, mechanics, chemistry, etc. The company then sent employment offers to universities which selected and recommended seniors for the positions and sent them for interviews. This was a common practice in many Japanese firms.

In selecting candidates through employment interviews, the company examined not only the applicant's academic performance, specialized knowledge, or particular skills, but, most importantly, checked his potential for development into a capable engineer or businessman within the company. In particular, the company emphasized the need for personalities which would work well with others and fit into the overall corporate culture.

The majority of the 27 engineers stated that they selected Tokyo Electric as their employer because the company was recommended by their university academic advisers. The engineers emphasized that this employment selection was almost automatic, and they did not consider it a major part of their career development process.

One of the engineers expressed the general feeling of the group:

> When the supervising professor of my thesis told me that he was considering recommending me for a job interview with Tokyo Electric, I did not know the company well. The only thing I knew was that the company emphasized business rather than the technologies themselves. My father encouraged me to join the company because my professor said it was a "good" company.

As with most Japanese university students, the engineers tended to be more interested in the company they selected as a whole than in a specific technological job. This tendency seemed to be caused by the relatively low interfirm mobility rate among employees in large Japanese companies and by the fact that larger companies provide better financial benefits and higher social status. Therefore, the engineers felt it was a natural step after graduation to join a large company such as Tokyo Electric and to be loyal to it for a lifetime.

Here is how one engineer expressed his feeling of loyalty to the company when he decided to join it: "I thought 'Ah, this is the company I will be working for for a lifetime' when I entered the west gate to hand in personal documents for recruitment. I promised myself that I would work hard to make this company better."

Introductory Education and First Placement

Every April 1, an entrance ceremony is held at Tokyo Electric. The day before, all unmarried recruits had moved into dormitories for unmarried junior members in the headquarters area. The company's policy is that all unmarried recruits must live in dormitories for the first few years in order to become accustomed to the company, learn basic rules and practices of the company, and develop a sense of group unity. Senior members in the dormitories were particularly important resources.

For a few weeks after the entrance ceremony, the new recruits attended a full-time introductory education program.[2] Its underlying emphasis was on establishing a feeling of permanent membership with the company and strengthening loyalty. During the first half of the program, the top management lectured on the company's philosophy of the spirit of unity and mutual help, and talked about management principles, such as the responsibility of the manufacturer to contribute to society through production. Various systems of administration based on lifetime employment were explained briefly. Tours to typical factories were made during the second half of the program.

In spite of this introductory period, the engineers interviewed did not develop a clear understanding of working under lifetime employment. One of the engineers recalled his experience during the introductory education program:

> Listening to lectures on the company philosophy at the headquarters education center made me feel as if I were still a university student. But the biggest concern in our dormitory was what jobs we would be initially assigned to. I spent a lot of time talking about this with dormitory mates, trying to develop a real image of the work we would do. When the practical training program began after I was placed in the division, I at last got a sense of "real work."

First placement of recruits occurred immediately after the introductory education program ended. To facilitate placement, the HRM department collected information on recruits' preferences in first task assignments through employment interviews. However, placement decisions were primarily based on the rotation and placement plan approved by a committee consisting of a top HRM executive and group executives in each business area. This plan was developed to consolidate demands for experienced engineers and new graduates.

Usually, the placement annoucements stated only the division or laboratory assignment. Specific first task assignments were determined within each division or laboratory by the head of that organizational unit.

The majority of the 27 engineers focused on in this exploratory study were placed in one of the three organizational units: Research and Development Laboratory, Lighting Division Group, or Small Appliances Division Group. However, some were initially placed in other areas and later transferred to one of the three units.

Upon placement in the laboratory, the new engineers were immediately assigned research and development tasks. On the other hand, engineers placed in the product divisions were required to attend several months of practical training programs in the factories to learn about the products and production facilities of the divisions. After this, they received their first assignments in engineering, such as sales engineering and product development.

Because the first placement, as well as later transfers, did not usually take individual preferences into consideration, the assignment of interesting jobs to the engineers was fairly random. Some of the engineers received interesting first task assignments; others did not. The engineers thus learned very early that one of the important aspects of lifetime employment is that the employee does not have the right to select his task assignments.

The engineers who were assigned interesting first tasks typically stated that they had ample opportunities to apply in a practical way the specialized technological knowledge and skills they had learned in their universities. Although jobs were assigned by their supervisors and general guidelines were set, the engineers felt they were largely responsible for their work. One engineer said:

> In my first task assignment, I solved big production problems of divisions by applying techniques of industrial engineering. That's my area. These problems were very important to the increase of productivity. For example, I substantially improved the productivity of a factory without investing money in facilities.
>
> I thought "This is a terrific company that gives responsible jobs to new members." I was attracted by the company through these experiences.

This engineer was able to see the products manufactured on the directions of the design drawings that he made. This was an exciting experience that he had never had in his university.

On the other hand, the engineers who were assigned uninteresting first tasks unanimously complained that they could not use what they had learned in their universities. In the laboratory, some of the engineers did not find any academic stimulation through assigned research projects. Other engineers in factories of the divisions received jobs which were not sophisticated enough for their specialized technological backgrounds. They wanted jobs more appropriate to their knowledge and skills. One of them explained:

> I was placed in a design section of electric switches in a local factory. Most people in the section had only a high school education background and they did not know how to use young members with a university background. My job was the hardware design of switches. But I did not find a way to use the theoretical knowledge I had learned in the university. These people placed a higher priority on their experiences rather than on theories. I was not satisfied with my job.

However, the assignment of an uninteresting task at the first placement did not necessarily lead the engineer to think about leaving the company. The abovementioned engineer continued to explain:

Although I was not satisfied, I did not think about quitting because I knew there were other places in the company where I could use my technology. In the introductory education program, I had learned from a lecture by the director in charge of technology that the company provided jobs in various technological areas, which included my area. I thought I was placed unfortunately in a factory which did not provide a suitable job.

During the 10 years focused on in this chapter, 1957-66, the 27 engineers interviewed worked at the nonmanagerial level in the organization without a major promotion. In this period of time, several first-line, technological tasks were assigned to most of them through transfers usually without considering their wishes. Their early stages of career development with the company were composed of performing these tasks. However, there were some engineers who continued to perform the same first task assignments until after 1966.

The engineers considered a shift from one task assignment to another through transfer as a career turning point. Usually this shift created a substantially different task assignment. Although they sometimes experienced a minor movement within one task assignment, they did not regard this as a career turning point. The movement did not create a new task assignment, and was often created by the merging of similarly functioning sections.

Task Assignment Situations in the R&D Lab

Task assignments of the engineers in the R&D Lab were first-line, technological activities of research and development projects. They were junior members of laboratory sections, each of which consisted of a section manager and usually four or five members. Sometimes, a senior member with the title of assistant professional supervised junior members' research and development projects. The engineers reported in writing monthly to their supervisors on the progress of their projects. Also, they presented oral progress reports at laboratory-wide monthly meetings with the top manager in attendance. In addition to those formal reports, they usually kept their supervisors informed on a daily basis.

Project topics were assigned by the section manager or accepted when members proposed them. In either case, the length of a project was a few years. Types of project topics varied from analytical basic research to product planning and development.

The major factor of the engineer's motivation and satisfaction in a first-line research and development project was the effectiveness of his strategic use of technological knowledge and skills to successfully complete a project.[3] While he was also pleased when the results of his project were applied in production, he felt more rewarded when the results met his technological expectations. An engineer explained how he had conducted a project:

> The project was the analysis of a chemical compound in order to identify its key component. It was anticipated that it would influence an important characteristic of a new product. First, I established a strategy of analysis to examine a number of components one by one.
>
> It's impossible to know at the beginning of a project if the strategy is good or bad. Often, it is only after one-third of the planned period of the project is completed that the strategy is found to be successful or not.
>
> I went ahead step by step in the analysis, carefully following and revising the strategy. When I identified the key component at last and it was what I expected in the strategy, I felt I succeeded in verifying the strategy. This was a great satisfaction to me.

Because the engineer was the person who conducted the project, he was able to directly know the progress and results of the project. This information demonstrated step by step how effectively he used his technological knowledge and skills in the analysis. The accomplishment itself showed his technological competence.

The purpose of first-line research and development projects is usually to generate the technological information that is required in wider or more important activities in the laboratory or divisions. Therefore, these projects do not provide many opportunities to make visible contributions to the company.

However, important projects were occasionally assigned to some of the 27 engineers and they were able to impact on the major corporate results. These projects were considered "in the mainstream" of the laboratory. Here is an example:

> I was first placed in a product division. A year later, I was transferred to the laboratory in order to join an important new product development project, in which I took charge of the development of an electric component. I had created its basic idea when I was in the division.
>
> I reported my progress directly to the top manager of the laboratory any time I felt it was necessary. He often rejected my design drawings and I had to redesign them many times in order to meet the high standards of the electric characteristics. Also, I reported to the division general manager every week. He taught me that products will not sell even if they are based on good technologies. In business, I have to consider costs, investments, and so on in addition to technologies. I was developing an important component which would create profit for the company.

In performing mainstream projects, engineers had to use more human relations competencies, along with technological ones, in order to effectively communicate with related people, who were usually higher ranked managers within and outside of their section. The great potential importance of these projects to the corporation generated business concerns among such managers.

On the other hand, while performing various research and development projects, some engineers came to realize that certain technologies or products tended to be considered "less important" in the laboratory. In such a case, even if the engineer successfully completed the project, he would derive satisfaction only from the technological accomplishment itself, since such projects rarely impacted on the major corporate results. One of the engineers explained his experience:

> My project in the assignment was the development of a new product using a particular electronic tube. I thought that it was better to use a transistor than the tube when I received the project from my section manager. But I did not say so, and decided to go with the tube. Because I was a young member, I wanted to be successful in establishing some patents for application with that kind of tube.
>
> When I successfully finished the project, the manager simply took the test product to a product division in order to propose the production of the new product. But the proposal was rejected because the division had already decided to use transistors for new models of that product.
>
> I should have used transistors, going with the technology trend. But I trusted the manager's decision to use the tube. I did not anticipate that the application of the tube itself would be turned down. I did not know that other sections had started similar projects using transistors, which were now the dominant technology.

Basic research projects, such as the analysis of materials, were likely to be perceived as "less important" and less visible in contrast to development projects of electric products, which were emphasized and "in the mainstream" of the company. This, of course, does not necessarily mean that engineers with less important projects were dissatisfied. In fact, the accomplishment itself of such a project did provide great intrinsic rewards to the engineer, as explained before. Furthermore, even in the areas of electric technologies, there were less important technologies being used, as in the example of the electric tube.

Task Assignment Situations in the Lighting Division Group

The majority of the engineers in the Lighting Division Group had performed first-line sales engineering jobs individually at local sales offices before 1966. They were the only members with engineering backgrounds in those offices.

Under the supervision of a sales section manager in a sales office, the engineer called on customers of lighting equipment and systems, such as design offices and construction companies. These calls were to generate customers' interest in the company's products and to help sell the company's products in the building construction industry.

To encourage customers to purchase the products, the sales engineer emphasized the technological advantage of the products and provided engineering support. Usually, one sales engineer performed several similar jobs at the same time. The length of a sales engineering job from initial contact with a customer until the purchase agreement was often a few years.

At first the engineers strove to learn about specific lighting technologies and equipment which were sometimes out of their technological specializations. They soon realized, however, that their clients' acceptance of an offer was based on strategies within their technological knowledge areas. Therefore, the sales engineers were motivated and satisfied essentially by the progress of jobs according to their strategies. One explained:

> Based on the information I obtained from construction plans by large companies and local government officials, I selected promising design offices as potential contractors. Then, I made many calls on the design offices as well as the companies and the government officials.
>
> When I called on customers, I carefully checked how they had considered my previous bids, and then I presented new ones according to my strategy. I also maintained human relationships with them. Trust is the key to business. Based on these factors, if necessary, I revised the strategies.
>
> I always knew if my sales engineering jobs were going well or not. When a job developed as planned in the strategy, I was on the successful track. When an offer was finally accepted, I was satisfied. Because there were competitors, this attainment meant the success of my strategy.

Although sales engineering jobs created profits ultimately through customer contracts, the engineers were more motivated and satisfied by the successful implementation of their sales strategies and the attainment of contracts than by the potential profit contribution to the company. This seems due to the fact that first-line sales engineers did not have responsibility for profits, as did the sales section managers.

Task Assignment Situations in the Small Appliances Division Group

The engineers in the Small Appliances Division Group mostly had product development assignments before 1966. They developed, or sometimes improved, various models of small appliances, such as hair dryers, in one task assignment. Typically, an engineer had two or three models at a time to develop, and it took less than one year to finish one model.

Section managers assigned development or improvement jobs to the engineers. They typically received design pictures of new models and their required electrical and physical specifications for development. Or they received specifications expected to improve characteristics of existing models. Based on these specifications, the engineers designed and assembled components. They reported job progress weekly to their managers and discussed deadlines, required levels of quality, and costs.

Their key job satisfaction came from developing and assembling an original product. One engineer described this feeling:

> After a designer gave me a picture, sometimes with a wooden model, of the target product to develop, I worked rather independently. While I informed the manager of the important points of my development strategy, he usually gave me only general suggestions.
>
> The most difficult point of product development was originality in selecting and using technologies. In other words, that was the source of the interest of the job. The selection of a new technology was always risky. I had to successfully study how to "practically" use it in a particular product within the assigned time frame. That was a challenge of developing an original product.
>
> When the developed product was manufactured in the factory and I received a sample, I was really pleased to see the product work as I had designed it. Sometimes I went to retail stores to see how my product attracted people.

The engineers stated that they became aware of the importance of relationships with people in successfully accomplishing their jobs. In the process of development, they depended inevitably on several people from related sections for various supports. For example, the manufacturing section developed test products according to their design drawings. Furthermore, they had to negotiate specifications, deadlines, and costs with the product planners, industrial designers, and their supervisors. The engineers realized that human relations competencies, along with technological ones, were required to get their jobs accomplished.

An engineer explained the importance of developing these skills:

> I found the management of personnel was difficult but important in my job. For example, there was a stubborn person in the factory, but I had to ask him to make a test product. When I took design drawings to him, I always had a difficult time making him agree to run a production test. Because he had his own jobs, human relations skills were needed to get him to squeeze my request into his schedule. I developed these skills after working on several development jobs.

Transfers

In the ten years between 1957 and 1966, the majority of the engineers experienced several transfers that they regarded as turning points in their early stages of career development with Tokyo Electric. Their task assignments substantially changed after each transfer.

While various corporate circumstances usually generated these transfers, individual career preferences were rarely considered.[4] These transfers were often made to meet the immediate needs of business and organizational development.

One of the engineers eloquently expressed how the company transferred individuals against their wishes. In his case, he was transferred from the headquarters to a local sales office in order to increase the number of sales engineers in the area. He explained:

I was surprised when the section manager gave me a notice of transfer to a local sales office. I was given only a week's notice to move to a new city that was hundreds of kilometers away from the headquarters area. He said my assignment at the sales office was for three years, and then I would be transferred back to the headquarters.

But, because I did not like sales engineering jobs, I asked him to cancel the transfer. Nothing happened. So, I went to meet the top manager of the lighting division to directly request the cancellation. He said he would think about it later. Then I was transferred. I worked there for seven years, not for the three years the section manager had promised.

Although transfers were based essentially on organizational and business concerns, the engineers were not always transferred to less interesting tasks. While the preceding example was of a transfer to a less interesting task assignment, the following describes another transfer to an interesting assignment, still without consideration for the individual's career preferences:

I was sent to a large foreign electric company to study their management of the sales engineering organization for one year. At that time, Tokyo Electric was considering how to streamline their sales engineering activities, which were being conducted in a rather unorganized way. My task was to learn and bring back the necessary knowledge. This foreign company was the leading one in this business area. I was selected for this task, I think, because I had a construction engineering background and some experience in living and studying abroad.

When I received the transfer notice, the marketing of a new product that I had been developing for almost two years in the previous division was just beginning. I strongly wished to continue that product development job. But the transfer notice was given to me as an order, and I could not voice my wish to my manager.

I soon learned that this transfer decision had been jointly made between the top managers of my previous division and the lighting division. Although the transfer itself was against my wish, this information encouraged me. I felt I was being chosen as a select member to establish a new sales engineering organization. Because lighting technologies were largely related to construction engineering, I was not switching to a completely different area.

In order to facilitate transfers, the HRM department provided many staff services. Using the centralized personnel records, it prepared a list of appropriate candidates who had the required competencies and backgrounds to meet division specifications. Furthermore, the department had input into the transfer plan and its related organization development plan in order to keep seniority-based promotion consistent.

Because transfers were originated primarily by division needs, young members usually had no opportunity to obtain jobs outside of their organizational units. To cope with this problem, the HRM department in 1963 launched a company-wide program of planned transfers of young employees with university backgrounds. The purpose was to help them develop their careers by giving them experience in various jobs in different divisions and laboratories.

However, individual preferences seldom held top priority even with the help of this program. In selecting candidates for the planned transfer program, the HRM department had to first take into account the division's or laboratory's manpower conditions. Managers there did not want to let their skilled engineers leave the department. And often, the engineers were transferred out of a department before they felt ready to leave.[5]

Some engineers experienced planned transfers. One of them expressed his feeling upon being transferred as follows:

> I was transferred from a product division to the Research and Development Laboratory. The Department of Human Resource Management made me experience different jobs outside of the division. But I was very disappointed in this transfer because I wanted to develop my career in the product division and I preferred product-oriented jobs rather than research-oriented ones. Anyway, I had to make a great effort to switch my way of thinking from the practical to the theoretical.

At the first placement after the introductory education program, some of the engineers received a task assignment in organizational units other than the R&D Lab, the Lighting Division Group, or the Small Appliances Division Group. However, by 1966, after several task assignments, they were interdivisionally transferred to one of these three units. Thereafter, they remained in that unit until the time of my interviews.

Outcomes

Through performing first-line, technological jobs until 1966, the 27 engineers interviewed learned several important things that helped develop their careers in Tokyo Electric Co., Ltd., and facilitated their understanding about working under lifetime employment.

One of the most essential points they learned is that because of frequent transfers without consideration of individual career preferences, striving to master the new technological skills and knowledge necessary for each task assignment is the key to job satisfaction at the first-line level. In Tokyo Electric, the technological career areas were generally defined to include all members with engineering and scientific backgrounds. Therefore, transfers in these areas often took engineers to jobs that required technological skills and knowledge out of their specialization fields. Because effectiveness in using technological competencies determined their satisfaction in first-line jobs, engineers had to master the new task competencies as quickly as possible after each transfer.

The engineers often expended great energy after each transfer in learning new skills and knowledge. One engineer described his feelings when he was transferred from an applied research project to a basic research project in the laboratory:

> I was too concerned about how to effectively perform the new task assignment to think of its importance to my career development. Because I had developed practical technological competencies very well during the previous project of applied research, it was really difficult to transform them to the new basic analytical research project.
>
> I worked very hard attacking analyses. Although I was forcing myself to think more theoretically and I didn't hate the new task, I couldn't go as fast as I expected. Particularly, when I analyzed a new material that had not previously been studied at all in the laboratory, I was extremely busy and found it very difficult to study the theory from A to Z.

Even when engineers were transferred to less interesting task assignments, the dissatisfaction was sometimes neutralized by the high level of activity and the great amount of effort required in learning and performing the new tasks. The engineer who was transferred to a sales engineering task at local sales office against his wishes explained what he had experienced:

> Because I was the only sales engineer at the sales office, I was truly busy dealing with everything related to engineering and technology. I learned lighting technologies through making calls on customers, explaining our products, and making technological calculations and design drawings.
>
> I was too busy to think that I didn't like that job. I had no time to think if it was interesting or not. I believe I must have been dissatisfied because I remember I often spent my free time with my office friends grumbling about the job.
>
> I did not intend to quit. I knew I would be transferred again sometime in the future, maybe to a more interesting job. I occasionally expressed my wish for a retransfer to managers at the headquarters in order to express my dissatisfaction in the previous transfer.

The engineers stated that they also learned that unsuccessful completion of tasks never leads to termination under lifetime employment. In fact, poor job performance was not unusual among the engineers. They sometimes failed to meet new product deadlines and consumed excessive monetary and manpower resources in creating malfunctioning components in product development projects. As young members, they worried that these unsuccessful results would lead to their employment termination.

However, when the engineers informed their supervisors of their failures, they were unexpectedly encouraged to tackle the next job even harder. The supervisors said that the company considered the unsuccessful expenses necessary for their development. The engineers thus learned that the company's policy was for young members to take risks and not to worry if they should fail.[6]

One of the engineers in the Small Appliances Division Group presented a typical example of a failure, which did not lead to termination:

> When I test assembled all components into a hairdryer which I had been developing, and I turned on the switch, no air came out of the dryer. At that time, I had full responsibility for that development job because my supervisor was fully committed to another job. Because all necessary molds I designed were made and ready to manufacture that malfunctioning product, I realized I had made a serious mistake. Fifteen million yen had already been invested in those molds.

I thought I would be certainly terminated. Anticipating my termination, I reported my mistake directly to the division general manager. But without saying a thing about termination, he really encouraged me not to think of the failure too much and to take time to successfully develop the product.

A few years later, this engineer successfully developed an efficient small electric motor, and the motor became a leading component for hair dryers manufactured in the division.

Although the engineers learned through experience that they would not be terminated under lifetime employment, they were never informed about performance appraisals, salary determinations, or transfer and promotion opportunities until they were about to be promoted to the section manager level.[7] The company did not seem to consider it necessary for the young members to know such matters because salaries and ranks were automatically incremented based on seniority until the employee approached the section manager level.

The final important point the engineers learned from performing various task assignments was that some products and parts of the organization were considered as "in the mainstream" of the company, and some were regarded as "less important."

As already examined, particularly in the section of task assignment situations in the R&D Lab, some of the engineers experienced mainstream projects. They had more opportunities to make major contributions to the company than other engineers with less important projects, and they used more human relations and technological competencies.

This awareness of the difference in importance between task assignments is also identified in the two product division groups. One of the engineers in the Small Appliances Division Group expressed his concern about being assigned to a less important task: "My target product of improvement was minor in the division. I worried that I would not make a visible contribution to the company. I envied my friends who joined the company at the same time as I did, and whose jobs were the development of the main products of the division."

Usually, supportive task assignments for the maintenance of the organization were regarded as less important and did not attract corporate attention, even though they were certainly needed to sustain the activities of the mainstream tasks. One of the engineers in the R&D Lab described this situation:

My task was developing and establishing equipment for other people's research and development projects. Although I thought this was very important to their experiments, the preparation of equipment was perceived as an undemonstrative background job.

I was never informed about the end results of the experiments because my job ended when I finished the equipment and delivered it to the client. Sometimes, let's say once every six months or once a year, I accidentally learned about the effectiveness of my previously developed equipment, for example, in a meeting with a top manager.

The awareness of being assigned less important jobs, however, did not necessarily discourage the engineers because the accomplishment of these first-line technological jobs was their essential source of job satisfaction. Sometimes, they had very challenging opportunities even in minor task assignments. One of the engineers had this experience:

> When a new product development task was assigned to me, I thought performing this task would not help me advance in the organization. The target product was somewhat inharmonious with the dominant products in the company. But I found I was really motivated in the job because I was the leader of the development. I understood entirely the technological characteristics and the marketing information about the new product. I was highly interested in developing the product.

This chapter has examined the 27 engineers' early stages of career development with Tokyo Electric Company. While the engineers generally understood they were exchanging lifetime employment for corporate loyalty upon entrance to the company, they realized after initial placement at the nonmanagerial level that real job satisfaction came from technological accomplishment in specific task assignment situations. Through performing various first-line technological tasks, they first learned about working under lifetime employment: striving to master new task competencies was the key to job satisfaction in each task assignment because individual career preferences were usually never considered in transfer decisions. Furthermore, the engineers became aware that certain emphasized product lines and parts of the organization were considered as "in the mainstream" of the company and others were regarded as "less important." Mainstream tasks were more likely to provide opportunities to make a major contribution to the company and required more use of both human relations and technological competencies.

6

The Engineers at the Mid-Career Stage:
1967-78

This chapter deals with the process of the 27 engineers' career development at the mid stage, and examines how their relationships with the company grew integrated. Their mid-career stages overlap between 1967 and 1978. During this period, the engineers were promoted to the section manager level, their first major leadership position. They developed their careers with the company through performing technologically managerial tasks as section managers or assistant professionals. All the engineers had entered the transition to the late stage by 1978, and became 40-45 years old in that year.[1]

Promotion to the Section Manager Level

Mostly through seniority, the majority of the engineers had attained the rank of NMJ4, one rank below the section manager level, by the beginning of the 1967-78 period. (See fig. 8, chap. 4.) They perceived that their promotion to the section manager level would be based more on seniority than on merit, especially since the merit system was based on performance appraisals which placed an overriding emphasis on seniority. In fact, when the engineers spoke about their advancement in the company, their consideration was limited only to their same-seniority echelons.

One of the engineers expressed his expectation for being promoted to the section manager level as follows:

> Before promotion to the section manager level, I thought much more about transfers to interesting tasks than about performance appraisals. I knew the performance appraisal created slight salary differences with coworkers in the same-seniority echelon. But the amount was very small and I didn't care about it.
>
> When my seniority approached the promotion age, I compared my speed of advancement with my fellow engineers and found I was a little behind. But I fundamentally expected my promotion during the next year because one-year seniors I knew were promoted that year. I thought I would have my turn next year.

All of the engineers interviewed were promoted to the section manager level (section manager or assistant professional) by 1972, after going through a promotion process administered by the HRM department. While the identification of managerial abilities was officially emphasized during the promotion process, its fundamental purpose was not to select employees with specific abilities, but to educate promotion candidates that they were receiving their first major status recognition in the organization.

For the most part, the engineers felt their nomination as candidates (by their superiors) for the section manager level was a natural and almost automatic step in their career development under lifetime employment, since the only requirements for the candidacy were seniority and satisfactory performance at the NMJ4 rank.

The latter requirement meant that a candidate had to receive a record of integrated performance appraisal scores above a certain level. Because the engineers were rarely told their scores, they were not certain that they had passed this requirement until they received their candidacy notices. Furthermore, an integrated performance appraisal score was calculated from very general and broad categories, such as "general evaluation of job performance throughout the year," "knowledge in the job area," "analysis and planning abilities," "judgment," "human relations skill," and "personality." These categories were so vague that it was almost impossible to know how to meet the performance criteria.

After becoming candidates, the engineers were required by the HRM department to take a part-time, six-month training program within the company.[2] During the program, they attended lectures on management skills, wrote research papers, and took psychological and managerial tests. The HRM staff interviewed each candidate about his career interest in managerial or professional jobs.

Although the HRM department emphasized throughout the program that the candidates' skills and personalities would determine their promotion, the engineers felt that the satisfaction of the seniority and performance requirements at NMJ4 rank were the ultimate determinant. All of the engineers interviewed were promoted to the section manager level.

One of the engineers in the Lighting Division Group simply stated his feelings after promotion as: "I thought I had become a section manager as a natural result of seniority. I was old enough to be promoted."

Immediately after promotion, the engineers were enrolled in a two-day education program within the company. Directors in charge of administration, technology, accounting, human resources, and marketing spoke to the newly appointed managers and professionals. There were also lectures on the management of labor relations and the mechanisms of personnel administration. It was usually here that engineers learned for the first time how job performance was appraised and how salaries and bonuses were determined.

The abovementioned engineer continued to say that: "I learned in the education program for the first time that seniority was not the sole determinant of promotion. I'd never imagined supervisors appraised my performance before. When I was promoted, I really thought it was because I had put in my time."

Promotion to the section manager level, the first major leadership position in the organizational hierarchy, was a significant career event for engineers in Tokyo Electric. With this promotion, the 27 engineers entered the mid stage of career development under the conditions of lifetime employment.

Task Assignment Situations in the R&D Lab

Each newly promoted engineer was titled an assistant professional in the Research and Development Laboratory. (No one in the laboratory was promoted from the NMJ4 rank to section manager because a laboratory section was organizationally at the same status as a division department.) The title of assistant professional in the laboratory held the same organizational status as the position of section manager in divisions. While an assistant professional did not have managerial responsibility for his laboratory section, he was expected to lead and be involved in research and development projects. He usually supervised one project at a time, but although he was the leader, his tasks were more technological than managerial. In fact, his work was highly involved in first-line technological activities with project members. The ultimate responsibility for the project belonged to the laboratory section manager to whom the assistant professional reported.

The number of members varied from project to project. When the project was requested by a product division and only its technological aspect was expected to be dealt with in the laboratory, the project team usually consisted of three or four members. When the project was jointly established with product divisions in order to develop a new product, it sometimes included more than 30 people to cover test production and quality examination.

As a project leader, the assistant professional was expected to calculate the expected profit contribution of the project (projected sales minus projected costs of research, development, and production.) The assistant professional also wrote monthly reports on the progress of the project, which he presented in laboratory-wide monthly meetings with the top manager and laboratory section managers.

The essential job satisfaction for the assistant professional was derived from the verification of his research and development strategy by the successful completion of the project. Because he worked closely with junior project members performing direct technological activities, his intrinsic job satisfaction was derived in the same manner as when he was at the nonmanagerial level.

It should be emphasized, however, that it was at this assistant professional level that the engineers stated they perceived most clearly that projects were either "in the mainstream" of the company or "less important." Mainstream projects usually dealt with electrical and related contemporary materials and technologies and were directly related to the development of a new product or technology. The projects were also expected to make major contributions to corporate profits and technological advancement and were highly likely to have explicit support from top management.

On the other hand, less visible supportive projects, such as basic material analysis and experiment facility development, were considered less important in the laboratory. These projects did not usually provide major contributions to the corporate results and tended to attract less attention from top management.

One of the engineers presented a typical example of a mainstream project as follows:

> The laboratory top manager assigned me a joint project with several product divisions to develop a new electrical device. At that time, the company was implementing a strategy to successfully compete with the major leaders in the market. The new device was expected to be the key competitive product.
>
> I was really excited working with many members with various technological backgrounds from divisions. The top manager provided us with more than enough financial and manpower support. He was also very helpful in negotiating with the divisions for technological and business aspects of the new product.
>
> At last, we successfully developed the new device. Customers really appreciated the product. This contribution to the corporate profits turned the expected profit contribution figure I forecast at the beginning of the project into a reality. I felt that I was creating the future of the company during the project. I was extremely satisfied and motivated by this major impact on the company.

An engineer assigned to a less important project described his experience:

> I started a basic analysis project of an alloy of several metals with a few members. I knew this was not a HIGH technology in the laboratory. Although I thought this alloy itself was certainly a fundamental material for the company's business, I had no realistic feeling about the expected profit contribution of this alloy. But I had to force myself to think that I was doing the essential thing for the company.
>
> Because this project did not produce visibly useful interim results for businesses, I had a hard time when I reported the progress of the project at the monthly meetings in the laboratory. The top manager wanted more directly useful results, so he advised me to terminate the project.

Although this case illustrated the worst result of a less important project, engineers assigned to such projects usually enjoyed great intrinsic rewards from first-line technological activities when they successfully completed the project. Another engineer explained:

> My project did not attract much interest from the top managers because it used a fairly new technology that was far away from the dominant technologies in the laboratory. I knew it would be miserable to try to impact on the top managers with this project, so I encouraged project members to appreciate each other's technological contributions to the accomplishment of the project. I eventually found the technological accomplishment itself was the great motivator and satisfier in that project.

The most significantly different aspect between mainstream projects and less important ones was the necessity of human relations competencies. Mainstream projects required assistant professionals to be more competent at coordinating and cooperating with related people. Because of the inherent importance of mainstream projects, these projects involved a variety of people from many parts of the organization, and their leaders were required to deal effectively with these related people.

An engineer explained how he used human relations skills in conducting a mainstream project:

> I had to introduce a large computer system in order to completely redesign the key component of a small appliance. Because this was a big investment, I really needed to persuade many top people. This was not an easy job.
>
> I carefully thought about how to induce them to accept the importance of the computer and the new design. Because the laboratory top manager, my section manager, and I were graduates of the same university, I had the advantage of being able to talk informally with them. I first successfully persuaded them, and then the top manager began to strongly emphasize the importance of my project at a variety of top meetings. Originally, I was, in a sense, imposed upon this project by the laboratory top manager, but I had to also "use" him to push forward my project. I also tried hard to develop informal friendly relationships with top managers related to my projects.

On the other hand, assistant professionals with less important projects did not need to use many human relations competencies. Because of their supportive nature, professionals were not supposed to visibly emphasize the importance and the high priority of these projects.

Task Assignment Situations in the Lighting Division Group

The engineers in the Lighting Division Group[4] performed mostly the tasks of sales engineering, product planning, and quality examination through transfers between 1967 and 1978. They were section managers, and their tasks were essentially to increase their sections' profits through effectively coordinating the technological activities of their subordinates.

The task of managing a sales engineering section was assigned at the local sales offices. Such a section typically provided technological information and services about the division's lighting equipment and systems for customers, such as construction companies and design offices, in order to persuade them to purchase products for construction projects. The section manager handled both administrative and first-line sales engineering jobs, giving approximately equal time to both. There were usually fewer than 10 subordinates in a section.

When the section manager performed a sales engineering job himself, his target was always a large construction project. One of the engineers gave an example: ·

> When I learned that a banking firm planned to establish a new headquarters building, I thought it would not be easy to get the bid because there was already a competitor in the group to which the bank belonged. It was common for a member company to get the bid from another member company in the same group.
>
> While our company did not deal financially with that bank, I knew our parent company had large dealings with it. So, I arranged with our group companies to bid for the purchase of products from our group companies as a whole. We successfully got the 500-million-yen order from the bank. But this order was not for the sole purchase of lighting equipment from Tokyo Electric.
>
> The next step I took was increasing our division's share of the 500-million-yen order. I used my relationships with the design office which contracted for the construction of the headquarters building. Furthermore, I called heavily on the electric construction companies to promote the increased use of our division's products for that building. My technological knowledge was very effective in emphasizing the better qualities of these products.

The engineers as section managers of sales engineering stated that they received great intrinsic rewards from the accomplishment of first-line sales engineering jobs. Furthermore, because their first-line jobs were usually large, job accomplishment often became a major profit contribution to the company and increased their intrinsic satisfaction.

The increase of the sections' total **profits** by their effective management of subordinate sales engineers also **provided** them with a sense of accomplishment. The results of their sections' contributions were shown in the internal financial reports, which visibly demonstrated their major impact on the corporate results.

One of the engineers described the key aspect of managing his sales engineers as follows:

> The most crucial task for a section manager was judging at what stage the subordinate's target construction plan was and deciding how frequently and on whom he should make calls. The frequency of calls on construction companies and design offices must be changed

according to the planning stage of the target construction project. Furthermore, the sales engineer must contact different people in each stage.

I exchanged information constantly with subordinates to identify the final stages of their target construction projects. That stage was the most crucial period. Both the decision on the plan and its order were usually made in the final week.

My section's profit marked 65% of the total profit of the sales office. That was a very, very good figure because the average was only about 45%. I was really encouraged by that figure, because it demonstrated my contribution to the company.

It was also important for section managers of sales engineering to effectively handle interorganizational relationships with other parts of the sales office and the parent lighting division. The sales engineering section was interdependent in the company, and the successful accomplishment of tasks depended largely on the human relations competencies of the section manager and his staff. Another engineer explained:

I had to keep good communications and friendly relationships with the order processing section in the same sales office. Their administrative work went faster than our technological work of drawing designs and calculating engineering figures. This gap of handling capacity became a big problem, particularly when many bids were accepted in a short period of time. Because they could not deliver products to customers as soon as they wanted, they began to fight with us. We were working as hard as possible. I had to get them to understand our capacity.

Furthermore, I had to deal with two bosses: the general manager of the sales office and of the lighting division. When the division requested the marketing of its new product line, and the sales office was not willing to deal with that, my effective communication and coordination skills became crucial. I really needed to cope successfully with such a managerial conflict because the product might be assigned to my section and I would have to make it profitable. I believed my efforts would contribute ultimately to the company.

The management of a product planning section was assigned in the headquarters of the Lighting Division Group.[5] The essential task of a section manager was managing his subordinates with first-line product planning jobs and maintaining external relationships with related sections for the subordinates to work effectively.

The task consisted of making a new product plan through creating and describing a new product concept and defining its technical and cost specifications. After this, designers sketched the new product, product development engineers designed its hardware, manufacturing people test-produced it, and quality examiners checked it. The product planner had to effectively coordinate all of these activities in order to bring the new concept to a finished product.

Because subordinates were the direct job performers, the section manager depended essentially on them to meet the section's product planning goals. He needed to use many human relations competencies to effectively coordinate their activities, and technological and product knowledge to trigger their initial creation of the new product's concept.

One of the engineers explained the typical process of subordinate management as follows:

> When it was decided that the marketing of a new product would begin in May, this product had to be cleared with the New Product Committee in March. I had to schedule product planning around that date. Coordinating activities among subordinates was the key to meeting this schedule.
>
> I met regularly with each of my subordinates during scheduling. Because they carried out plans, their understanding of and input into the plans were the key factors in successful completion of the product. I also encouraged them to research competitors' products, technology trends, consumer preferences, and so on. I felt it often more difficult to trigger their creative thinking than to coordinate the activities. I made a lot of daily face-to-face contacts with them to monitor their progress. I checked technological and cost specifications and made sure designs and test products were completed.
>
> I frequently stopped by related sections such as product development, production, and quality examination to help my subordinates get their cooperation. It was the engineers in these sections that actually materialized my subordinates' new product concepts. I had to foster and maintain cooperation from their section managers.

The engineers as product planning section managers acquired great motivation and satisfaction from originating the ideas for all of the company's future products. When their sections created a successful new product which contributed to the corporate profits, they felt rewarded. This visible and concrete impact on the company strongly showed their competence in management. However, the engineers did not feel the same satisfaction in completing each component of a product planning item, since they could not see the impact it would have on the entire finished product. (This motivation and satisfaction will be clearly illustrated in the next section of this chapter.)

The task of managing a quality examination section was also assigned in the headquarters of the Lighting Division Group. The major task of such a section was examining the quality of the new products developed in the division group. Most of the section members were manual workers with first-line jobs of operating examination equipment to test product quality according to standard procedures. The task of the section manager was to motivate workers and to oversee quality control in cooperation with related product planning and development sections.

Although the section manager's task was typically managerial, its accomplishment made neither a visible nor a major contribution to the corporate results, due to the supportive nature of quality examination. One section manager gave this explanation:

> Every month, my section received about 10 items to examine for electrical and physical qualities. When the examination results did not meet corporate standards, the product was returned for improvement. Because a new product was usually planned and developed

along a tight schedule, our request for improvement was often perceived as spiteful behavior by the product planning and development sections. Although the identification of imperfections before marketing was our goal, it was never appreciated, and usually construed as a block to the smooth progress of new product planning and development.

Many new products were often scheduled to be marketed in the same month. One month before, we always had a rush of re-examinations that was the result of our previous requests for improvement. When we did a good job, we only made our jobs even harder.

The task of quality examination was perceived as less important and rewarding than product planning and development, which provided many more opportunities to visibly contribute to the company. The task attracted less attention in the technological process of manufacturing business. The manager continued to explain:

The task accomplishment of quality examination never rewarded me. The product planning and development people ultimately initiated each task, and I had to cooperate with them. I didn't want to hear their grumbling: "What will you do about the delay in marketing this product because of your request for improvement?"

Task Assignment Situations in the Small Appliances Division Group

The engineers in the Small Appliances Division Group[6] became section managers of product planning, product development, and production mostly through transfers between 1967 and 1978. Their tasks were to attain the section's goals through effective management.

Management of a product planning section in this division group is essentially the same as that in the Lighting Division Group just examined. The engineer as a section manager in the division group coordinated subordinates' product planning activities and managed relationships with related sections such as product development and quality examination.

The key job satisfaction of the section manager was the creation of new business for the company. Through effective management, he could develop a successful new product and make a major contribution toward the corporate profits.

One of the engineers acting as section managers explained his interest in the product planning task:

I created the basic concepts for the leading products in my division. These would never have been put on the market if I had failed in the crucial phases of coordinating my subordinates' activities with related sections such as product development and quality examination. My satisfaction and motivation came from the accomplishment of such coordination and the origination of the company's business.

People think that a new product is created by a designer. They don't know there is a product planning manager who generates the concept and manages the process of its materialization. The difficulty of the task is to get engineers, designers, and even top managers to understand the concept and why the new product is needed in the market.

The management of a product development section was also assigned to the engineers in the Small Appliances Division Group. As with the product planning section, management tasks here were essentially in coordinating subordinates' activities and maintaining external relationships with the related sections. Because the section goal was to develop hardware, however, the engineering aspect was much more emphasized in management. The manager materialized the product from its concept, cooperating with sections such as product planning and quality examination.

One of the engineers described his managerial task in product development as follows:

> When a new product concept was established in the product planning section, I joined them to discuss and examine the whole process through test manufacturing. I assigned its development to one, or sometimes more than one, of my subordinates, who created engineering designs to meet the specifications defined by the product concept. I usually worked with them to select proper technologies and materials for its engineering. In my section, 10 to 15 items were always going.
>
> One of the most difficult points of my job was meeting the development deadline. By a certain date, the development of a new product had to be completed and ready for the market. It was a hard job for a manager to encourage and accelerate subordinates' engineering activities. Sometimes, I worked directly with them to help solve technological problems in engineering.

The management of relationships with related people was also an important job for the section manager of product development. Another engineer explained:

> I had to communicate effectively and cooperatively with a variety of people from a molding engineer of an outside supplier to an equipment operator of the quality examination section. The most crucial point in communication was the timing. When I asked them something before the circumstances became ripe, my request didn't go smoothly. So, I tried to create conditions for generating the timing. When I hit it, everything went very well.

The engineers as product development section managers stated that they were highly motivated and satisfied by establishing the hardware for new products. Even though the concepts were usually generated in product planning sections, the engineers developed them into real products to be used in society. They felt greatly rewarded by visibly contributing to the company through physically generating profitable products. One of them explained his motivation:

> I was really interested in using new technologies and materials to develop products. The true competitiveness of products came from this risky engineering challenge. People in the research and development laboratory could never think about how valuable new technologies or materials are on the market. We were creating their value through the difficult process of engineering and complicated interactions with the related sections.

The engineers in the Small Appliances Division Group experienced the task of production management through transfers at the section manager level. They were managers of production sections with from 120 to 200 workers, mostly women. The managers had some foremen in their sections, too.

The key task of production management was meeting monthly production plans provided by the production control section. For this purpose, the section managers had to effectively control workers' production activities weekly, daily, and even hourly when necessary. They were required to use many human relations skills to keep workers highly motivated.

One engineer stated the importance of human relations competencies:

> My target was not materials or technologies but human beings. Because my workers were women with junior high or high school educations, I had to carefully select and use words which were understandable to them.
>
> I taught my workers quality control techniques from the beginning for the two purposes. One was to have more communication opportunities with them. While teaching, I had a kind of teacher-student relationship with them rather than a supervisor-worker one. The other purpose was to give them a sense of control over their assembling jobs and to help them cope with the monotony of repeating defined actions at the same speed. Using quality control charts, I was able to help them understand control points of their jobs and they became careful in assembling to clear these points. But I had to be patient with them because their learning was slow. I had to go along with them.

The engineers as production section managers were greatly satisfied by accomplishing production plans. Because worker motivation was not constant, supplies were changed, and facilities were not perfect, this accomplishment demonstrated their high managerial abilities. One of the engineers described how he derived satisfaction from managing his section under these changes:

> My daily efforts to motivate the women were rewarded particularly when new production facilities were successfully installed without affecting production speed. During the actual installation, our production of components had to stop. But the next production section which uses our components in their assembly could not wait for our production to resume. So my section began producing more than the daily schedule so we could pool the required amount of components to be used during the production stoppage. I felt greatly rewarded when we successfully attained this amount before the stoppage. I thanked the women for their extra efforts.

Transfers at the Section Manager Level

The majority of the 27 engineers were transferred several times during their tenure at the section manager level (section manager or assistant professional). They performed substantially different jobs after each transfer, and considered each one as a turning point in the mid stage of their career development with the company.

Because the organization rarely considered individual wishes in transfer decisions, the engineers were often transferred to task assignments that required technological knowledge and personal skills which they had not acquired previously. As they had experienced at the nonmanagerial level, they had to strive to learn the necessary knowledge and skills as quickly as possible at this level. In order to increase the sections' profits or to attain the projects' goals, the engineers were required to effectively learn and use both technological and human relations competencies in working with subordinate engineers, who often had more technological knowledge and skills than their superiors.

At the same time, through transfers some of the engineers tended to have more mainstream opportunities to develop human relations competencies and to make a major impact on the corporate results than others.

In the R&D Lab, some of the engineers with electrical and related technological specializations were more likely to be assigned mainstream projects, which had clearly defined relationships to the important electrical products in the company, than were engineers with peripheral specializations. This meant that the mainstreamed engineers had more opportunities to develop human relations competencies and to visibly contribute to the company.

In the Lighting Division Group and the Small Appliances Division Group, however, most of the engineers tended to experience both mainstream and less important task assignments. As previously examined, sales engineering, product planning and development, and production management were regarded as in the mainstream; quality examination was considered less important. Because the number of engineers in a product division was limited and because the use of technological knowledge and skills was less complicated, technological backgrounds were not usually considered in transfer decisions in divisions. Therefore, most of the engineers in the division groups had frequent mainstream opportunities and developed human relations skills.

One of the engineers interviewed in the R&D Lab explained this tendency:

> Particularly in the late years at the nonmanagerial level, I was really motivated with research and development projects in which I converted brand new important electronics technologies into commercial products. I realized the importance of human relations skills to effective job performance. Because this was a new area, I had to talk with many high-ranking people to get them to understand the technologies' promising potentialities for new products.
>
> After I was promoted to assistant professional, I conducted many projects to solve system design problems using computer system techniques. These problems were originally too difficult for the division engineers to handle in their development of new products, such

as new lighting systems in the Lighting Division Group and very sophisticated small components of appliances in the Small Appliance Division Group.

Because the division engineers spoke different languages based on their technologies, I had to first learn their technological jargon as well as to carefully modify my system technology terms when speaking to them. Furthermore, I had to present my system solutions in careful steps, so as not to scare them. Usually, they resisted switching to a new system. I had to make a strategy of explaining the benefits of my system designs to them.

Through these experiences, I developed good human relations competencies. I became able to determine how much I could say formally, and what I should say through informal means. Furthermore, I learned how much I could emphasize my points and how much I should accept another person's points in negotiations.

The system designs I made always became big and successful contributions to the development of the new products because no division engineer had solved these system problems before. I was extremely satisfied by the large corporate attention to my accomplishments. One of the new products was mentioned highly in the newspapers, and I and my subordinates were honored by the president at a company-wide annual meeting.

Another engineer in the laboratory who performed only less important projects gave his point of view:

> Almost all of my task assignments at the position of assistant professional were minor and small projects with very new technologies that were different from the dominant contemporary technologies in the laboratory. But I did not care how other people considered the results of the projects. I was really interested in discussing technological and theoretical points with my subordinates.
>
> I was satisfied because I did what I was interested in. Although the results never made major contributions to the company's profits, I did not think about it. I knew my project team was isolated, but I was motivated to research new technologies that other people didn't understand. I was the person to do that.

On the other hand, in the Lighting Division Group and the Small Appliances Division Group, the engineers were likely to have a combination of mainstream and less important task assignments through transfers. An engineer described this transfer tendency:

> Because I joined this company to work for a lifetime with loyalty, I am willing to perform any kind of job. In fact, I have always experienced both major and minor jobs. Every three years, I think, I had an opportunity to make a major contribution to the company.
>
> When I was assigned a major task which enabled me to fully utilize my specialized technological knowledge and skills, I was really motivated to demonstrate my competence by accomplishing the task. My successful development (of a really new appliance) was a good example of the result of this motivation. The top people of Tokyo Industry, our parent company, appreciated the fact that Tokyo Electric created the new product. I felt I made an impact on the company. I realized that my self-confidence increased in that way.
>
> When I was assigned a minor task which required technological knowledge and skills out of my specialization, I used this assignment as a good opportunity to learn. I worked very hard in such a task.

> After I became a section manager, my self-confidence increased by effectively managing subordinate engineers who essentially carried out first-line technological activities. The development of my human relations competencies became more important.

In the divisions, the development of human relations competencies was made usually when the engineer experienced a mainstream task assignment. One of the engineers there explained how he developed these skills in performing sales engineering jobs:

> When I was transferred to a sales office, I found for the first time that a sales engineering section depended upon many other sections to accomplish its goals. I had to develop cooperative relationships with people both in the sales office and headquarters. For example, when we accepted a large construction project which needed specific lighting equipment that the division did not provide, I had to establish a cooperative network of division engineers for the successful development of that equipment. I was required to use many kinds of human relations skills in order to make that network function to facilitate the development.

Another engineer also discovered the importance of human relations competencies and learned them when he was transferred to a product planning section:

> I realized that the management of product planning was the management of the process from product concept generation to manufacturing. Human relations competencies were required much more than specific technological knowledge and skills, which were used in certain phases of that process by first-line engineers. I had to make all sections of product development, manufacturing, marketing, etc., work cooperatively. I learned how to develop and use cooperative relationships among necessary people. Because the task of product planning management went beyond formal organizational relationships, I had to rely on these human relationships.

By the end of the time period focused on in this chapter, 1978, about 70% of the 27 engineers had been promoted to the department manager level (department manager or principal professional). An examination of the promotion process of these engineers is given in the next chapter.[7]

Outcomes

The 27 engineers interviewed for this book had spent between 17 and 21 years with Tokyo Electric Co., Ltd., by the end of their tenure at the section manager level, or by 1978 if the tenure lasted beyond this year.

The engineers' integrating relationships with the organization had developed into either active or passive organizational involvement. Although all the engineers remained loyal to the company, some of them became actively motivated to make great contributions while others developed relatively passive attitudes to the organization while contributing minimally. These appear to be the positive and negative resulting attitudes from the engineers' experiences which occurred through transfers: performing only mainstream or less important task assignments, or performing a combination of both.

As examined in the previous section, some of the engineers in the R&D Lab were more likely than others to be assigned mainstream projects. Because of this, they became actively involved in the organization. They had more opportunities to make a major contribution to the company by effectively using human relations as well as technological competencies. Their successful accomplishments often led to visible and concrete establishments of new technologies and products, which provided major profits for the company. The engineers were highly motivated by these demonstrations of their competence and this intensified their active involvement in the organization.

On the other hand, the engineers with less important projects developed a relatively passive attitude toward organizational involvement. Because the results of these projects were essentially supportive and less visible, the company provided only limited attention to their effective use of competencies. This encouraged the engineers to passively relate their task performances to wider business activities in the company and to make minimum efforts only within the technological areas of the projects.

However, when engineers successfully learned and used new technological skills and knowledge required in newly assigned, but still minor, projects, they did not necessarily remain passive. In fact, they were often greatly motivated and satisfied by the accomplishment of first-line technological activities with subordinates.

In the Lighting Division Group and the Small Appliances Division Group, the engineers were likely to be transferred both to mainstream and less important task assignments. They became actively involved in the organization because they frequently experienced mainstream opportunities to impact on the major corporate results throughout their sequence of task assignments. However, this active involvement was created only when they successfully continued to learn new technological knowledge and to develop human relations competencies in order to effectively manage subordinates and maintain relationships with the related sections.

One of the engineers in the R&D Lab provided a typical description of active involvement in the organization after performing all mainstream projects as a assistant professional:

> I was conducting a series of product development projects in order to establish a major electrical product line in the company. The laboratory top manager and the division general managers always directly told me to identify and include promising future technologies in

the current projects. They emphasized how to integrate these technologies with the company's future business.

I was really encouraged to contribute to the company by originating future business. I worked hard with my project members to examine the potentials of new technologies. At the same time, I collected and analyzed information about customer needs and market characteristics. Cooperating with division people, I integrated the information into new product concepts.

Afterwards, my task was essentially to present the laboratory top manager with ideas about future technological trends and how to integrate them into research and development projects in the laboratory. I was greatly motivated to develop ideas about how to increase the research and development effectiveness of the laboratory as a headquarters technology center in order to originate future business.

In contrast to the above engineer's development of active organizational involvement, another engineer provided a typical example of developing a passive attitude toward involvement through performing mostly less important projects:

My task as an assistant professional was leading projects that measured electrical characteristics of materials and products which were made in other parts of the laboratory. The purpose of these projects was not simply to filter out materials and products with imperfections but to research why they were bad and recommend how to improve them. In essence, I was cleaning up technological troubles made by other people. This was an unrewarding job. Why did I have to take care of other people's failures?

My interest in these projects quickly decreased. In fact, the technological problems I dealt with were often very difficult, and the original engineers could not have handled them. Furthermore, the job did not provide me with a sense of mission. I didn't feel I was contributing to the company by technologically helping the other people's projects get completed successfully.

I continued the job simply because that was my assigned job. I forced myself to understand that there was no one except me to perform the job, but I was using only physical energy to perform the job.

However, as illustrated in the previous section, the first-line technological accomplishment even of a less important project could provide great intrinsic rewards. Therefore, when the engineer continuously performed less important projects and successfully learned and used new technological knowledge and skills required in each project, he did not necessarily develop passive involvement in the organization. He could still be motivated and satisfied with first-line technological activities.

Another engineer explained how he coped with learning and using new technologies and how he led it to job satisfaction:

I had been performing research and development projects in the area of organic chemistry, such as the analysis of synthetic resins, before I was promoted to assistant professional. But the promotion took me to the area of nonorganic chemistry, which was out of my specialization. After this, I conducted, as a leader, many projects in that technological area. While both organic and nonorganic chemistry were not mainstream technologies in the laboratory, that switch was the greatest change in the process of my career development with the company.

In order to cope with this switch, I decided to become an engineer who dealt with both areas of chemistry. In fact, such an engineer was almost nonexistent in the company. I studied nonorganic chemistry very hard while performing projects with young members. Also I set up the goals of the nonorganic chemistry projects to identify organic resins that easily adhered to nonorganic materials. By doing this, I focused on the interacting areas between the two technologies.

Although nonorganic chemistry projects were rarely related to major product lines in the company, I became interested in these projects by applying both organic and nonorganic viewpoints. I was motivated by multiple-technological approaches.

On the other hand, in the Lighting Division Group and the Small Appliances Division Group, the majority of the engineers interviewed developed active involvement in the organization through frequent mainstream opportunities. One of them described typical development of identification with the company as follows:

The basic characteristic of my motivation had, I think, changed before and after my promotion to a section manager. Before the promotion, I performed technological jobs, which means I used my knowledge and skills. But, as a section manager, I motivated my subordinate engineers and other people outside of the section to work to attain my section's goals. This means I was using the section's and the related parts of the company's organization.

I found it greatly interesting to use the company's organization to impact on the corporate results. I experienced transfers through which I had to learn new skills and knowledge required in the new task assignments. That was a really hard job but very important to attaining the section's goals, which often became major profit contributions to the company. Technological knowledge and personal skills were essential to effectively motivate subordinate engineers.

After performing several different tasks at the section manager level in the division, I came to think that I became a section manager in order to change and create the organization of my division into one in which I could perform more effectively to impact on the company.

However, in the division groups, there was an engineer who failed continuously to learn new technological knowledge and to develop human relations competencies. He did not become actively involved in the organization. He explained:

I was transferred to a product development section, for which I assumed responsibility a year later. This section dealt with some lines of custom-made products with technologies that were completely new to me, but I had to learn these new technologies in order to increase the section's profits. Furthermore, I ordered my subordinates to call on potential customers to get as many orders as possible.

More lines of new products with new technologies were added some years later. It was very difficult to learn new technologies at the same time as performing the jobs. But I met the section's profit goals somehow or other.

But, when a recession came, orders for my products decreased quickly. I tried to get more subordinates to make more calls and to receive more orders. But my request for human resources was turned down. So, I didn't meet the profit responsibility, and was transferred to another section as an assistant professional without profit responsibility. But the new technologies I had previously acquired did not apply to products in this section, either.

I think my career development at the section manager level was only in learning one new technology after another. I did not feel any business accomplishment from meeting profit responsibilities. I felt that assigning people to one new task after another without setting clear career directions did not help them to develop. I began to think that I related to the company only by learning a new technology and performing a job using it. I was repeating this piece by piece during my career development.

The 27 engineers interviewed for this book entered the mid stage of their career development with the company upon promotion to the section manager level. While the promotion process reinforced their feeling of all-encompassing membership with lifetime employment, the engineers now occupied their first major leadership positions in the organization and began to concretely contribute to the company. However, the engineers realized more clearly at this level that task assignments were either "in the mainstream" in the company or "less important." Furthermore, some of the engineers tended to be assigned more mainstream tasks than others. By developing more human relations and technological competencies, these engineers contributed more to the major corporate results and developed active involvement in the organization. Because of limited opportunities to make a visible impact on the company, the other engineers developed a passive attitude toward the organization.

The Engineers at the Late-Career Stage: 1979-82

This chapter is the final part of the trilogy on lifetime employment relationships and integration between the individual and the organization. The purpose of the chapter is to examine how the 27 engineers interviewed for this book further developed and reinforced their active or passive involvement in the organization after they had developed these attitudes, as examined in the previous chapter, at the section manager level in Tokyo Electric Company, Ltd. Between 1979 and 1982, these engineers performed purely managerial task assignments at the department manager level. These managerial performances constituted the late stage of their career development under lifetime employment, and they became 44-49 years old in 1982.

Promotion to the Department Manager Level

By 1978, the engineers had met certain seniority and performance requirements at the section manager level and had been promoted to the assistant department manager level, one rank below the department manager level. This promotion essentially meant that they would be promoted to the department manager level. Engineers in the company usually performed jobs at the assistant department manager level as training for jobs at the department manager level, or they were directly promoted to the department manager level from the section manager level. Furthermore, no training program was provided for promotion to the department manager level beyond what was provided at the assistant department manager level.

The promotion process to the assistant department manager level was quite similar to that to the section manager level described in the previous chapter. Its fundamental characteristic was again the emphasis on the company's expectation of the individual's all-encompassing and close relationship with the organization. The engineers were recommended by their laboratory or division top managers as candidates for promotion when they met certain seniority and performance requirements. These requirements were as general and as wide-ranging as those considered for promotion to the section manager level. The satisfaction of these requirements was the essential determinant for promotion to the assistant department manager level.

The headquarters Department of Human Resource Management required candidates to take a part-time, three-month training program within the company, which was similar to the program for promotion to the section manager level. Candidates attended lectures on managerial skills and abilities and wrote research papers in the program. Furthermore, the HRM department conducted psychological and managerial tests and interviewed each candidate. Although the identification of higher-level managerial capabilities among candidates was the official purpose of the program, its essential emphasis was on reinforcing candidates' awareness of all-encompassing membership with lifetime employment.

Usually, promotion decisions were announced in December, and the newly appointed assistant department managers and associate professionals were required to take a two-day education program within the company. Directors in charge of administration, technology, accounting, and human resource management spoke to them about the importance of the department manager position to the company and its relationship to the company's philosophy.

Fewer candidates were promoted in the same year they entered the promotion program than at the section manager level. Many candidates had to wait several years. Promotional decisions were made by the Department of Human Resource Management in cooperation with division heads when new or vacated positions at the department manager level became available.

Merit was considered more heavily in promotional decisions at this level than at the section manager level. The promotion delay difference between "slow runners" and "fast runners" in the same-seniority echelon became much greater although the year of entry into the company was carefully checked by the HRM department in order to control very fast promotions. In fact, the number of years that the 27 engineers spent from promotion to the section manager level to the department manager level varied between 2 and 12, with the average at 7.3 years.

One of the engineers, whose promotion came quickly, compared his advancement with that of his fellow engineers in the same-seniority echelon:

> By checking company newspapers or other sources of information, I always knew I occupied a leading position in my same-seniority echelon. I also knew my ranking position as a result of the training program for promotion. Actually, I attained the earliest promotion to department manager in the echelon. I was not dissatisfied with the promotion system and did not feel any different when I attained my promotion.

On the other hand, even though his promotion was slow, another engineer had this thought about why he was promoted: "I thought I was promoted because I met the seniority requirement. I knew my performance at the section manager level was not very good. But I was not dissatisfied with it because I had worked hard and because I ultimately attained my promotion."

Promotion to the department manager level actually provided much more responsibility than that to the section manager level. Laboratory sections and division departments were considered profit centers in the organization, and decisions by their managers were necessarily related to corporate strategies.[1] Task assignments at this level were purely managerial, and the distance from the first-line technological activities became much greater.

Most of the engineers in the Research and Development Laboratory skipped over the rank of PJ2 as associate professional and were promoted directly from PJ1 to PJ3 as principal professionals or MJ3 as laboratory section managers. On the other hand, the engineers interviewed in the Lighting Division Group and the Small Appliances Division Group were appointed department managers after they spent a few years as assistant department managers. Their experiences at the assistant department manager level served as training for the department manager level.

Promotion to the department manager level provided a great advancement in terms of status and financial benefits. It was regarded as the highest achievement among nonmanagerial employees, who felt it demonstrated superior ability. The ranks beyond this level formed the top management level in the organization and promotions were handled by the Board of Directors, not by the Department of Human Resource Management.

The HRM department applied a uniform pay scale for the department manager level. This generated a great increase in individual monthly salaries and biannual bonuses over the section manager level. A HRM manager described these financial benefits: "Young members at the nonmanagerial level don't know how much department managers and principal professionals receive. Perhaps, it's impossible for them even to imagine it. If they knew, they would be very angry at the comparison with their small salaries at the nonmanagerial level."

Task Assignment Situations in the R&D Lab

Task assignments of the engineers interviewed in the R&D Lab were highly managerial regardless of the job title (laboratory section manager or principal professional). These tasks were of two types: the first was the management of a laboratory section, with the job title of either laboratory section manager or principal professional; the second was working as a deputy to a laboratory section manager, with the title of principal professional.

We will first examine the task assignments of the managers of laboratory sections. These managers set research and development projects and assigned them to assistant professionals or to first-line section members. To ensure progress in these projects, they had to deal with many managerial, instead of technological, details that related to the internal and external aspects of their sections.

One laboratory section manager presented this general view of the administrative jobs he had to perform:

> I attended many administrative meetings in the laboratory. Among these, the budget meetings were the most important. I was responsible for planning and overseeing my section's budget, and I had to get these budget plans approved in the meetings. Lots of preparation was needed. Also, I had to do a lot of administrative paperwork every day.
>
> Performance appraisals of my subordinates were another important job. It was very difficult to evaluate subordinates with less visible and slower-progressing projects.
>
> Because I usually did not deal directly with projects, I depended on progress reports from subordinates. I was far away from the first-line project activities and felt it difficult to encourage project members effectively. Yet, their motivation was a highly necessary consideration for me.
>
> Furthermore, coordination with other sections in the laboratory and related departments of product divisions was also important to the successful completion of projects.

The engineers who managed laboratory sections with many mainstream projects were greatly motivated and satisfied by making major contributions to the company. Because they had been performing mostly these kinds of projects since they were assistant professionals at the section manager level, they had well-developed essential human relations competencies.

One of these engineers expressed his self-confidence in managing his laboratory section as follows:

> The purpose of my laboratory section is creating ideas for new technologies and products and expanding the company's business. My task as a manager is to integrate technological ideas and activities by both junior and senior members of the laboratory section toward this purpose.
>
> I have an ability to watch and listen to subordinates and to help them be more creative. Also, I can utilize well subordinates whose ideas are creative and unusual. They are very important sources of innovation.

On the other hand, the engineers who had often conducted less important projects as assistant professionals tended to be appointed managers of laboratory sections with less important projects. In this case, however, they also lost the opportunity to get technological satisfaction from first-line activities since their jobs became entirely managerial. Because they had not had the opportunity to develop their human relations skills as assistant professionals, they often regretted their highly managerial assignments and would have preferred to remain at first-line research and development activities.

One engineer presented typical dissatisfaction with his assignment:

> When I was appointed laboratory section manager, I was very anxious about taking managerial responsibility for a laboratory section. I didn't request this assignment. I am not good at managing people because I have developed technological skills rather than personal ones during past projects. After performing managerial jobs every day, I feel it is important but very difficult to deal effectively with human relations and negotiations.
>
> I delegate almost all technological responsibilities for projects to assistant professionals. They report the progress of their projects to me usually with the figures from their experiments. It's impossible to control projects only through this indirect information. Actually, I cannot relate to the first-line engineers and effectively motivate them.
>
> I also have difficulty working with other laboratory sections. Because I have my own way of performing research and development and they have theirs, it's hard for me to cooperate with them.
>
> Honestly speaking, I don't like managerial tasks, and I'm not interested in them. Of course, I envy managers who have mainstream projects. Ours are less important ones that never provide concrete and visible contributions to the company. I'm trying not to allow this dissatisfaction to adversely affect my subordinates.

The second type of managerial task, which was performed by some of the engineers interviewed in the R&D Lab, was working as a deputy to a laboratory section manager. The company usually created a few of these positions for principal professionals in a large laboratory section with many research or development projects in different but related technological areas.

The deputy laboratory section managers worked as support staff to the laboratory section managers. They assisted them in planning research and development projects and provided technological advice to assistant professionals who actually led these projects. Although the deputy managers were in mid-management positions, they did not have direct technological responsibility for projects. The deputy managers stated that they felt dissatisfaction with their task assignments, especially when conducting less important projects.

One deputy manager expressed his feelings as follows:

> My assignment as deputy laboratory section manager is the biggest turning point in my career development in the company. The biggest is, however, the worst.
>
> I'm really confused with this job. How I can use my technological knowledge and skills in planning projects? The joy of material analysis, my specialization, is the detective work I use to search for the unknown components. I'm no longer a detective. I became an administrative planning officer.

Task Assignment Situations in the Lighting Division Group

The engineers in the Lighting Division Group had mostly managed departments, such as sales engineering, product planning, and quality examination, through transfers between 1979 and 1982. Because they were department managers, their jobs were highly managerial.

Managing sales engineering departments was assigned in the headquarters area and some major local cities in Japan. These departments were called the sales engineering headquarters in these areas, and the department managers were actually the heads of these headquarters.

Although the engineers still performed some first-line sales engineering jobs as department managers, their essential task was managing the sales engineering headquarters. They were responsible for the profits of the central or area headquarters and had to effectively manage relationships between sales and product divisions.

One of the engineers described the typical responsibilities of the sales engineering headquarters managers as follows:

> I have top responsibility for all sales engineering activities in this area. I make the final decision about tendering a proposal, and also make the final decision about potential construction projects after receiving input from my sales engineers or division personnel. My task includes formally answering complaints from customers in this area, too.
>
> Because the sales engineering headquarters are the middlemen for the area markets and the product divisions of the Lighting Division Group, I'm required to effectively provide appropriate marketing information to the product divisions. At the same time, I play the key role in coordinating selling and manufacturing activities and implementing product strategies of the divisions in my area.

Managers of the central and area headquarters interacted with a larger number of people in performing their tasks. They coordinated with many general managers and department managers of product and sales divisions, and occasionally the president and executive vice-presidents. They considered not only the interests of their own headquarters but also those of product and sales divisions.

One of the engineers told about having a dramatic increase in the number of people with whom he had to coordinate in performing his tasks, and the importance of effective management of human relations:

> When I was a sales engineering section manager, I had had only 5 or 6 people to interact with. But when I was promoted to the manager of this area sales engineering headquarters, the number of people I had to maintain relationships with increased to about 30 or 40.
>
> When I maintain good cooperative relationships with people, my job goes well. Because I have to work with both sales and product divisions, the most difficult part of the job is the complexity of using human relation skills with both them.

> For example, when my headquarters deals with one-billion-yen orders from some large construction projects, I have to coordinate many sections in sales and product divisions which are related to these orders. Requests about order handling from top executives tend to be higher because of the importance of external company relationships generated by accepting these large orders.

Engineers performing highly managerial jobs at the central or area sales engineering headquarters were greatly satisfied with their major impact on the corporate results. One explained this feeling as follows: "I am really satisfied with my ability to contribute to the prosperity of the company. The sales which the Lighting Division Group makes now occupy one-third of the company's whole sales. I am playing an important role in the marketing of lighting products."

The task of managing product planning departments was assigned in the headquarters of the Lighting Division Group. The department manager was required to manage the creation and implementation of long-term policies of new product planning and development. This was a highly managerial task based both on a long-range creative viewpoint and human relations competencies.

One of the interviewees explained the necessity of creativity and human relations skills in his managerial task assignment:

> The basic goal of my task is presenting long-range considerations and goals for new product planning and development, from which each of my section managers develops a six-month plan of activities for his section. For this purpose, I analyze trends of fashions and culture, and forecast how electric lighting will be used in the future. Creative thinking is needed to generate ideas to satisfy consumer preferences for lighting products, to preempt the competition, and to create counter-product strategies.
>
> Although these long-range policies are based on my original ideas, I take into consideration conditions and situations of other parts of the organization while planning these ideas. As a department manager, I have to consider how all products of the division will sell and how our product policies fit with other product policies in the company. I collect a variety of information through wide-range relationships with people in the organization. Establishing respect and goodwill in the company is the key success factor in this job.

The product planning department manager who implemented the long-range policies of product planning and development in the division relied largely on human relations competencies, too. Through these highly managerial activities and the others described above, he made major profit contributions to the company. This demonstrated his business accomplishment and greatly satisfied and motivated him. (These points are clearly illustrated in the next section.)

Managing the quality examination department was also assigned in the Lighting Division Group. Because quality examination supported the progress of product planning and development tasks performed in other departments, it was not regarded as being in the mainstream of the company.

The task of the quality examination department manager was also highly managerial: he coordinated activities through section managers and maintained effective cooperation with product planning and development departments. However, department managers were hardly ever motivated to perform this managerial task because they did not initiate the fundamental process from product creation to manufacturing and because they were not able to visibly demonstrate their competence through this process.

Anticipating the relative lack of importance of the task, one engineer became discouraged even before he actually started performing the task: "When I learned I would be promoted to a manager of the quality examination department, I was not pleased. I thought that the department would not be an interesting place to work because this kind of task was not at all exciting. I knew the necessity of quality control in a manufacturing business, but this was not the task I wanted to do."

Low job motivation produced minimum job efforts at the department manager position. The abovementioned engineer continued: "While working as the department manager, I only did the things that were requested by product planning and development departments with the highest priority. I had no reason to take care of everything, because I didn't initiate any of the tasks."

Task Assignment Situations in the Small Appliances Division Group

During the four years focused on in this chapter, the engineers in the Small Appliances Division Group were managers of a department, such as a product planning department or a product department.[2] Like the task assignments examined in the previous section, these tasks were highly managerial.

The management of a product planning department in this division group also required the use of creative thinking and human relations skills to develop long-range policies of product planning and development. To implement these policies, the manager had to rely largely on his human relations competencies, as described by one of the engineers:

> Although the general manager of the division "decides" product policy, its origin is in my product planning efforts. I have to somehow control him so he will not deviate from the basic idea of the policy in his decision making. Because he has the highest authority in the division, this is not an easy job. His performance is evaluated by the result of his decisions. So, he makes decisions based on his own judgment and takes final responsibility.
>
> In the hierarchy of the organization, it is impossible for a subordinate to persuade a superior completely to accept the subordinate's idea. I must, therefore, create an organizational and interpersonal situation in which the superior naturally accepts my idea

as his own. I force myself to be patient about the time-consuming and complicated activities which such a situation generates.

For example, when there is a conflict between my ideas and the general manager's over how to increase profits, I don't push mine. Instead, I promote discussions between him and a general manager of a sales division, who insists on a price-cut to boost sales. These discussions clarify that a price-cut will not produce a profit increase, and my general manager becomes eager to find another idea. I wait for a ripe opportunity to present my idea to him again. I need his willingness to understand an idea in order to persuade him to accept it.

Managing a successful product planning department often led to the creation of successful new products, which made great profit contributions to the company. Department managers were extremely satisfied and motivated by the major impacts they made on the corporate results. The engineer above explained: "My division's product lines occupy leading positions in the markets. I'm confident in my ability to contribute to the company, to my country, and to the world. I feel very pleased by the fact that a great number of people in this society use the products which my ideas created."

The task of managing product departments was also assigned to the engineers interviewed in the division group. Each of their product departments dealt with certain product lines and typically included sections of product development and production in its organization. The engineers were required simultaneously to control functions of product development and production management. Their managerial performances were evaluated in terms of sales of products and costs of manufacturing. These jobs were also highly managerial.

One product department manager described the managerial responsibilities of his job as follows:

I develop monthly and semi-annual production and selling plans. My target is to reach the sales and cost figures proposed in these plans. I have to report earnings and expenses of my department in monthly meetings with the general manager and all department managers of the division. My performance is evaluated in these meetings.

The most important resources for the attainment of profit goals are my subordinates. They are the ones who actually develop and produce the products and generate profits by selling them to the sales division. Having effective subordinates is the key.

Because of lifetime employment, it is almost impossible for department managers to fire unsatisfactory subordinates or employ engineers with needed skills and experience from outside the company. The engineers stated that when department managers requested that the HRM department allocate engineers from other departments, the department usually requested that the department managers accept new university graduates in a one-to-one exchange for their experienced engineers. This kind of exchange was very unacceptable because experienced subordinates were crucial for the everyday operation of the department and the release of an experienced subordinate was not equivalent to the allocation of a new graduate.

Therefore, department managers were required to be competent in developing and retaining effective subordinates within their departments. One engineer described his experience in "winning back" a capable subordinate:

> When I was promoted to assistant department manager and transferred to this product department, I found a promising young engineer among my subordinates. He was interested in learning a new technology. I really helped him master the technology, and then he became a leading engineer of that technological area in the company.
>
> Later, I was asked by the department manager, my boss, to release the young engineer for the manager's new task assignment in a different organizational unit. He was being transferred there, and I was taking over his department manager position. I accepted the request on the condition that the engineer be returned as soon as he finished his job in the unit.
>
> But such conditions were usually not met. A "temporarily" transferred engineer was soon considered a subordinate of the person who took him away.
>
> I used a variety of means to get him back. Finally, I submitted a proposal for the development of a new product and it was accepted. The proposed product promised to be very profitable to the division, but the transferred engineer and his technology were indispensable for its development. When my proposal was accepted, I made a formal request for my engineer to be transferred back. I successfully persuaded top managers of my division and the unit to send him back.

The product department managers stated they were greatly satisfied and motivated by the contributions they made to the company. Effectively managing the development and manufacturing of profitable products was the fundamental function of the product divisions. One of the engineers expressed his feeling about his job as follows: "Because my department develops and manufactures all products in this division, I actually generate the division's profits. I spend billions of yen in developing, manufacturing, and selling products to create profits for the company. That is a huge amount of money, which a small company president never deals with. This is a really interesting job."

It should be noted that the transfer experiences of the 27 engineers at the department manager level manifested the same characteristics that were identified and examined in the previous two chapters, although the time period focused on in this chapter is less than half as long. With each transfer situation, the engineers were usually required to acquire new technological knowledge and develop human relations skills for effectively managing their laboratory sections or division departments. Also, in the R&D Lab, some of the engineers were more likely to be continuously transferred to task assignments with mainstream R&D projects than others. In the Lighting

Division Group and the Small Appliances Division Group, the engineers tended to have a combination of mainstream and less important task assignments.

Outcomes

The subjects of this book had spent between 21 and 25 years under the lifetime employment system with Tokyo Electric Company by the end of the quarter-century study period in 1982.

The engineers' active or passive involvement in the organization, as identified in the previous chapter, developed more clearly after their promotions in the late-career stage to the department manager level. Experiencing purely managerial task assignments at this level fostered the discrepancy between these two types (active and passive involvement) of integration relationships between the individual and the organization.

Some of the engineers continued to perform mainstream tasks at the department manager level, which further intensified their active organizational involvement which had been initially developed at the section manager level. Because they had developed human relations competencies well in these previous task assignments, they were able to accomplish successfully their highly managerial tasks and to increase their motivation to contribute to the company.

At the same time, however, purely managerial task assignments generated a great distance from the first line of technological activities and eliminated opportunities to derive intrinsic satisfaction from the direct accomplishment of these activities. Some of the engineers who had initially developed a passive attitude to the organization while working at the section manager level became very dependent on lifetime employment for job security, while making a minimal commitment to their jobs. Because they had had few opportunities to effectively develop human relations competencies in relatively unimportant past task assignments, they were now unable to derive intrinsic satisfaction from either managerial or technological accomplishment.

In the R&D Lab, as already examined, the engineers who managed laboratory sections and who had been performing mostly mainstream projects had high job satisfaction and were motivated to make major contributions to the company. They became very actively involved in the organization. One expressed this attitude toward the company:

> The purpose of my laboratory section's projects is to generate information not only for use within the laboratory but for use in establishing and implementing corporate strategies. I set projects to deal with wide-range topics concerning the corporate administration of this company.

Using system design technologies, I quantitatively forecast technology, market, and economic trends. I'm trying to quantitatively understand cause-and-effect relationships between the company's business actions and the corporate results.

Because I have an electronics and system technology background, I don't want to compete with professors of business administration. However, for the sake of the company, I'm developing knowledge and skills in business administration based on the electronics and system technologies.

On the other hand, some engineers had been performing mainly less important research and development projects and had failed to adequately develop human relations competencies through their task assignments. These individuals were almost necessarily forced to take a passive role at the department manager level in the organization. One of these engineers expressed his attitude:

I was appointed deputy laboratory section manager, I think, because of my seniority. This section's projects are minor and less visible, but I am in charge of managerial aspects of these projects. I'm not interested in the administrative and political activities that are needed to deal with top managers or other laboratory sections. There is nothing to stimulate my technological interest.

I don't work very energetically. I process administrative requests only because they come from the laboratory administration section. I technologically advise assistant professionals only to meet the R&D management guidelines which were set by the top manager.

I perform these minor and uninteresting administrative jobs because of lifetime employment. Without worrying about termination, I work within these very limited areas.

Most of the engineers in the Lighting Division Group and the Small Appliances Division Group were greatly motivated and further intensified their active involvement in the organization through numerous mainstream opportunities in a combination of major and minor task assignments at the department manager level. One of these engineers stated his identification with the company:

I had been performing mostly sales engineering jobs since I joined the company. I had been the sales engineering manager in several local offices and the manager of some area sales engineering headquarters. Most of my career in the company developed as the sales engineering organization grew. I felt I have played an important role in the development and prosperity of the Lighting Division Group and the company.

Recently, I was transferred to a staff department, of which the management is, I believe, important to the growth of the division, but actually less visible than sales engineering headquarters management. My technological knowledge and skills as a sales engineer are rarely applicable to this job. But I am very motivated to perform this new assignment. Human relations competencies are the key to the successful accomplishment of this staff function.

I want to contribute to the company by effectively using my human relations competencies which I developed while performing sales engineering jobs. I thank the company for having let me enjoy these mainstream jobs and achieve my great career growth in the company. Now, I want to repay the company by managing this staff department to effectively support division activities.

This high integration between the individual and the organization in the divisions is based on the engineers' successfully and continuously acquiring technological knowledge and developing human relations skills. For some of the engineers, this was not possible, and they were unable to make a major impact on the corporate results. These individuals tended to develop a less active involvement in the organization. An engineer in this category expressed his passive feelings this way:

> Most task assignments I have performed in the division were too new to me. While performing these tasks, I came to think that it was better to work only within the given conditions with minimal effort.
> I think I have lost my ideals in work. I miss the excitement of the first-line engineering activities when I was a young member. I wish I were still just an engineer.

Active or passive organizational involvement among the 27 engineers interviewed was reinforced by the high status and good financial benefits provided at the department manager level. While these corporate rewards were the simple result of promotion and compensation systems based essentially on seniority with partial emphasis on merit, they tended to reinforce the engineers' active or passive attitude toward the company.

Engineers with active organizational involvement perceived status and monetary rewards as the company's recognition of their abilities and contributions. They felt encouraged to be more competent and contribute more. One of these engineers explained how he perceived the system:

> When I look back over my promotions and compensation increases, I think they reflect the effort I put forth and my successful accomplishments very well. Superiors watch who contributes to the company, and their judgment is accurate. Up to now, I have been successful in performing any kind of jobs assigned through transfers and attained a high status and salary. I feel confident this success will continue in the future.

Engineers with passive organizational involvement did not worry about their minimum commitment to the job leading to employment termination. They received lifetime job security in exchange for their loyalty to the company. Furthermore, their high status and good financial benefits encouraged them to stay in the organization without improving their attitudes. They did not feel guilty about this situation because they believed their passive attitudes were fostered by the company's human resource management practices such as transfers without consideration for individual career preferences.

One of the engineers eloquently expressed how he has come to depend on lifetime employment while giving minimal job efforts:

I have no intention of leaving this company. Because I have never thought about it, I have no outside job alternative. I don't know the value of my technological and managerial abilities in the job market. Probably, there is no job that will give me as much status and compensation as my current one.

I'll continue to work as I do now. I probably won't have interesting tasks in the future because I haven't had them in the past. I'm too old to feel a calling and a sense of mission in this kind of work.

The engineers' late stages of career development under lifetime employment began with their promotion to the department manager level. Although the promotion process to this level was quite similar to that to the section manager level, the engineers' task assignments became much more managerial. Performing these highly managerial tasks, the engineers intensified either their active or passive involvement in the organization, which they had initially developed at the section manager level. Some of the engineers with active involvement were again assigned mainstream tasks and further developed this attitude by successfully accomplishing these tasks and contributing greatly to the company. In previous assignments, they had already developed human relations competencies, which were essential to these highly managerial accomplishments. Other engineers with passive involvement, who had failed to develop human relations competencies previously, were unable to derive intrinsic satisfaction either from managerial or technological accomplishments at this purely managerial stage in their career development. They were almost necessarily forced to assume more passive attitudes toward the organization.

8

Conclusions and Implications

Conclusions

The major question my research sought to answer is: What integrating relationship develops between the individual and the organization through the process of career development under the Japanese system of lifetime employment? Although the managers with engineering backgrounds interviewed for this book remained loyal to the company, the following quotations typify their contradictory views:

> I have developed my career with this company through performing mostly tasks that allow opportunities to contribute to the company. I have always been aware of the significance my performance has on the corporate results, and my task efforts have led to successful product lines in this division. When I think about the future of my division, I am willing to assume major responsibilities in order to further develop the business. My way of thinking and my actions coincide exactly with the values of the company. [A product planning department manager, Tokyo Electric Company]

> When I look back over what I have been doing in the laboratory, I don't find I have any technological specialty which has given me self-confidence and career identity. I have conducted many technologically different research and development projects, and all of them have been undemonstrative and minor. But, lifetime employment has helped me get promoted to the level of department manager. I am satisfied with my current status and salary level. I don't need a salary increase, and there is no particular type of new job I want to do. [A deputy laboratory section manager, Tokyo Electric Company]

My research and the quotations above indicate that career development process under lifetime employment, which is understood as based on a relationship of exchange of mutual benefits between the individual and the organization, produces both active and passive organizational involvement. For some of the engineers interviewed, the condition of lifetime employment created a motivation to contribute as much as possible to the company; others depended on lifetime employment for status and job security while contributing only minimally to the organization. These are the positive and negative resulting attitudes of loyalty, which my research shows is essentially fostered by the Japanese system of human resource management.

This empirical evidence partially contradicts previous studies such as Ouchi's "Theory Z," which states that human resource management based on the Japanese system of lifetime employment creates high member involvement and, consequently, high productivity. My belief that this is a one-sided and overly simplistic viewpoint triggered the development of this book.

Some of the engineers developed active involvement because they successfully exchanged intrinsic rewards for effective job activities and accomplishments, mostly through task assignments that provided "mainstream" opportunities to impact on the major corporate results. They received high organizational status and financial benefits primarily with seniority in return for their career-long efforts to acquire new technological knowledge and human relations competencies in each new task assignment, regardless of their individual career preferences. The engineers' satisfaction with this exchange reinforced their active involvement in the organization.

Other engineers developed passive attitudes toward the organization after they failed to receive intrinsic rewards from performing mostly "less important" jobs which provided fewer opportunities to make a major impact on the company. Limited corporate attention to these less visible, supportive jobs afforded no opportunities for feedback about their contributions. These engineers were also often unsuccessful in developing necessary task competencies in new task assignments. In spite of this, however, they received seniority-based promotions and compensations, because the Japanese lifetime employment system basically exchanges corporate job security for individual loyalty.

The engineers entered the company after university graduation with the general understanding that in return for loyalty they could expect lifetime employment and job security. Through its introductory employee education program, the company emphasized its philosophy of unity and mutual help among employees and its expectation that the individual would develop an all-encompassing and close relationship with the organization.

The engineer's early stage of career development was comprised of performing first-line, technological task assignments at the nonmanagerial level without major promotions or formal feedback from performance appraisals. He was expected to work hard and take risks without worrying about performance results. In fact, through practical experience, the engineer learned that poor job performance never led to termination. Furthermore, he learned that he had to be willing to take on new task assignments because transfers were usually made without considering individual career preferences.

While the company provided uniform incremental rank and salary increases based on seniority, the engineer's motivation and satisfaction came primarily from accomplishing first-line, technological jobs although they did not usually make a visible impact on corporate results. The progress and results of his work directly demonstrated his technological competence and gave him intrinsic rewards. Because of this, the engineer learned that striving to master the new technological skills and knowledge necessary for each assignment after transfer was the key to job satisfaction at the first-line level.

At the same time, the engineer developed an awareness that certain emphasized product lines and parts of the organization were considered to be "in the mainstream" of the company. Task assignments in these areas were more likely to provide opportunities to contribute to the major corporate results and generated more intrinsic satisfaction. More human relations competencies, along with technological ones, were used to cooperate with related people within and outside of these areas because of the great potential importance of the mainstream task to the company.

There were also supportive task assignments necessary for the maintenance of the organization. While they were certainly needed to sustain the activities of mainstream tasks, they were regarded as "less important" because of their less visible results and because they received less corporate attention.

The engineer's entrance to mid-stage career development was through promotion to the section manager level, his first major leadership position. The company's expectation of the engineer's all-encompassing membership under lifetime employment was again demonstrated in this promotion process. The process was based on merit with an overriding emphasis on seniority and used general evaluation categories and criteria. Results of performance appraisals were not usually fed back at this level, either.

Through his new managerial position, the engineer was expected to recognize business and engineering realities and to contribute to the corporate results. His task assignments required that he demonstrate human relations and technological competencies in order to increase his section's profits. This direct contribution to the company, which was often reflected in the company's internal financial reports, provided him with a sense of business accomplishment in addition to first-line job satisfaction from performing technological activities with subordinates.

However, the relative importance of task assignments became more evident at the section manager level. In the R&D Lab, engineers with electrical and related technological specializations tended to be assigned mostly mainstream projects, while those engineers with peripheral specializations such as basic material analysis were likely to handle less important projects. In the Lighting Division Group and the Small Appliances Division Group, most engineers experienced a combination of mainstream and less important task assignments because of the limited number of engineers and because less technical knowledge and abilities were required. Mainstream tasks in these division groups were product planning, sales engineering, product development, and production management. Quality examination was perceived to be less important.

The availability of opportunities to perform mainstream tasks at the section manager level had an impact on whether the engineer received intrinsic rewards from task accomplishment and became actively or passively involved in the organization. Those engineers with mainstream projects in the laboratory identified strongly with the organization because they perceived their jobs as using both their human relations and technological competencies to make a major impact on the corporate results. Engineers with less important projects which made only a minor impact on the corporate results often developed a more passive attitude toward the organization. The limited attention by management to such projects provided no feedback about the effectiveness of their use of competencies to even indirectly contribute to the company. However, if these same engineers successfully learned and used new technological skills and knowledge, they often derived intrinsic satisfaction from performing technological job activities with subordinates even in minor projects.

Other engineers at the section manager level in the divisions gradually developed active organizational involvement because of frequent opportunities to perform mainstream tasks throughout their sequence of task assignments. However, this active involvement was realized only when they were able to continue to meet the company's expectation for learning the new technological and personal skills needed to manage subordinates.

The engineer's late stage of career development under lifetime employment began with his promotion to the department manager level. Because positions at this level of the organization were highly managerial, his career development here hinged on his performance of purely managerial tasks. Although promotion was again based essentially on performance appraisals with a wide range of general categories and criteria, it created a much greater distance from the first line of technological job activities. Also, it provided a great advancement in status and financial benefits over the section manager level.

Promotion to a purely managerial level boosted the emergence of both active and passive organizational involvement among the engineers. Engineers with mainstream projects in the laboratory were more likely to become actively motivated to make a major impact on the corporate results because they had had many opportunities to develop human relations competencies at the section manager level. However, some engineers with minor projects were almost necessarily forced to develop a passive attitude of involvement in the organization. They had had no prior opportunity to develop such competencies at the section manager level, and now they had no supplementary opportunity to get job satisfaction from first-line, technological activities.

In the division groups, active involvement in the organization was intensified by successfully learning new technological skills and knowledge after transfers, which simultaneously provided opportunities to develop human relations competencies. Those engineers who failed to develop new skills and competencies or did not make major impacts on the corporate results were less actively involved in the company.

Active and passive attitudes of involvement at the department manager level were reinforced by the benefits which the engineers received as a result of the reward system based on seniority with limited emphasis on merit. Engineers with active involvement perceived these organizational rewards of high status and good salaries and bonuses as the company's recognition of and encouragement for their contributions to the company. Others with passive involvement felt safe from termination because of the organization's basic underlying guarantee of job security in exchange for employees' loyalty. They did not feel guilty about contributing minimally to the organization because they perceived their passive attitudes as justifiable, since they had sacrificed their career preferences for the good of the company.

Based on this evidence of the development of either active or passive member involvement in the organization, it can be said that "Theory Z's" assertion of the advantage of the Japanese lifetime employment system for creating high member involvement and high productivity is one-sided and overly simplistic. The fundamental point of this theory is that the exchange of the employee's present performance contribution with the deferred acceptance of corporate rewards from the seniority-based long-term promotion and compensation systems leads to high integration between the individual and the organization. The results of this study indicate that this integration is successful only if the employee is able to exchange intrinsic rewards for effective job activities and accomplishments throughout his career development under lifetime employment.

Implications for Research

It is not possible, given the limited number of research subjects and the single company on which this exploratory study is based, to make a definitive theoretical or practical statement about integration between the individual and the organization under lifetime employment. But it is possible, based on the results, to provide useful suggestions to researchers and managers. In this section, I discuss the implications of this study for future research on integration.

For the most part, my findings support the exchange aspects of integration between the individual and the organization which were previously identified in the review of fundamental studies of integration. The general framework developed from that review has demonstrated its usefulness in focusing on the process of the individual's career development and his integration with the organization. Figure 9 is a summary of mutual expectations between the two parties which have been identified in this book.

However, two theoretical considerations for future research are indicated, one of which adds to the previous knowledge of integration through the exchange of intrinsic rewards for job accomplishments in job activities, while the other diverges from that of integration through the exchange of optimal challenge and performance evaluation feedback for the facilitation of intrinsic satisfaction in activities surrounding the job, such as human resource management activities of performance appraisal, transfers, and promotions.

First, the engineers in my study indicated that the intrinsic rewards they exchanged for job accomplishments at each stage of career development differed as their tasks at each stage differed. Previous research studies have considered intrinsic rewards such as a sense of competence and self-esteem to be uniform throughout the career development process. This study shows that when the engineers performed nonmanagerial technological jobs in their early-career stages, first-line technological accomplishments were their key job satisfactions. At the section manager level, or mid-career stage, the engineers were satisfied and motivated by the successful completion of technologically managerial tasks. With promotion to the department manager level, at the late stage of career development, the accomplishment of purely managerial task assignments was the engineers' source of intrinsic satisfaction. This evidence indicates a need to more precisely define the variable of intrinsic rewards throughout the career development process in future research of integration between the individual and the organization.

Second, my research indicates that performance evaluation feedback received through human resource management activities does not solely facilitate intrinsic satisfaction and motivation, as was previously expected. My findings show that while the performance appraisal system in Tokyo Electric did not formally provide feedback information to employees, the engineers received informal feedback from increases in status and financial benefits and other means. This informal feedback served two purposes: to reinforce active motivation in exchanging intrinsic rewards for job accomplishments, and to secure passive dependency on lifetime employment after failing to provide this exchange. This implies that performance evaluation feedback facilitates intrinsic satisfaction only when the employee is successful in exchanging intrinsic rewards for job accomplishments.

At the same time, this study indicates that the performance feedback

Figure 9.   A Summary of Mutual Expectations between the Individual
            and the Organization under Lifetime Employment

Individual Expectations

General:
        —lifetime employment and job security
        —promotion up to a point in the individual's career based on seniority
        —fair salary based on seniority
        —minimum performance evaluations up to a point in the career
        —opportunity to contribute to the company

Related to the Early-Career Stage (Nonmanagerial Level):
        —first-line, technological job accomplishments
        —use of the individual's educational background

Related to the Mid-Career Stage (Section Manager Level):
        —technological managerial job accomplishments

Related to the Late-Career Stage (Department Manager Level):
        —highly managerial job accomplishments

Organization Expectations

        —loyalty
        —unity and mutual help
        —all-encompassing and close relationships with the individual
        —willingness to perform any job without consideration for
          individual career preferences
        —willingness to take risks without worrying about failure
        —ability to strive to acquire new technological and human relations
          competencies in each task assignment
        —recognition of engineering from a business viewpoint

information that was provided directly by the progress and results of first-line technological jobs and by the company's internal financial reports of sections' and departments' results much more powerfully promoted the intrinsic satisfaction of the engineers who were actively involved than that by the HRM system. Furthermore, the minimal corporate attention to supportive jobs provided no feedback information to the engineers with these jobs and intensified their passive attitudes toward the organization. These findings appear to mean that there are other kinds of feedback mechanisms that facilitate intrinsic motivation, which is not considered in the previous studies. It is suggested that future research must focus more precisely on what feedback information promotes intrinsic motivation, and how.

In terms of methodology and research design, I have two basic recommendations for future research in integration between the individual and the organization under lifetime employment. First, a much broader quantitative study of integration must be made to develop a generalized conclusion for this study. This study indicates that a successful or unsuccessful exchange of mutual benefits between the individual and the organization throughout the process of lifetime career development impacted on the development of either active or passive member involvement in the organization. But, because of the exploratory nature of this study and the small research sample, this conclusion must be treated as tentative until a statistical study validates or disproves it. The general framework and the interview guides developed through this study can serve as useful tools for the development of a questionnaire to begin this quantitative study.

Second, it is necessary in future field studies to vary company and subject's occupation and promotion experiences in order to test the research evidence against the influence of industry, company climate, occupation, and promotion on the development of integrating relationships between the individual and the organization. This study's research design dealt with an electrical manufacturing company and 27 of its engineers who experienced two major types of promotion experiences (promotions to the section and department manager levels). These variables remained constant throughout the analysis.

As a final methodological consideration, the results of this study present a suggestion for further research about the Japanese style of management: to focus more on "real" work activities of Japanese people in organizations without overemphasizing "unique" cultural aspects of the Japanese management system. This suggestion could change the direction that research in this area has taken during the last quarter-century.

Intrigued by the initial research of Japanese factory organizations by Abegglen (1958), most researchers of Japanese management style since then have focused essentially on identifying unique characteristics of Japanese culture and management systems. These studies tend to emphasize the distinction between collectivity in the Japanese culture and organizations and the individual orientation of American counterparts. They credit the high productivity of Japanese firms to the uniqueness of Japanese lifetime employment and related personnel systems based on that collectivity, discussing their effectiveness in facilitating subtle communication and collective decision making in organizations. This research direction has culminated in Ouchi's "Theory Z," which my research evidence has described as one-sided and too simplistic.

That empirical evidence has become available not by focusing excessively on unique cultural aspects of the Japanese management system but by dealing essentially with actual work relationships and interactions between the Japanese company and the employees. I closely examined real task assignment situations provided by the company, and the employees' actual activities and motivation there. Previous research studies have tended to conceptualize solely the cultural aspects, and were therefore very abstract and did not analyze the "real" work activities of people in organizations.

By focusing more on the actual activities of people in organizations, we can research differences among Japanese companies that could never be analyzed through the cultural approach. Comparing effective and less effective Japanese companies will help more precisely understand how the Japanese management system functions. Furthermore, this focus will make it possible to analyze the differences and similarities in successful management of Japanese and American companies.

Implications for Management Practices

The central message my study has for managers, particularly for American managers, is that the Japanese style of management is not a panacea through which the individual's integration with the organization can be increased and high productivity can be attained. So-called "Japanese management" studies, such as "Theory Z," do not always represent the problems of the lifetime employment system. The empirical evidence presented in this research shows that Japanese lifetime employment and related human resource management systems can develop high involvement and motivation among employees, but there is a potentially crucial drawback: these systems may simultaneously foster employee dependence on lifetime employment and job security while exacting only a minimal commitment to the job. The expected high productivity by actively involved members may be neutralized by the low effectiveness of employees who have a passive attitude toward the organization.

This drawback of lifetime employment is commonly referred to as the

"Large Company Disease" in Japanese business society. I encountered many Japanese companies where productivity is actually threatened by this "disease." Furthermore, even in the U.S., high-performing corporations which have reportedly adopted Japanese-like long-term employment commitments to their members may be expected to have the same problems in the future.

However, it should be emphasized that both Japanese and American managers with long-term employment commitments can successfully join more passive employees with actively motivated employees to achieve high integration between all members and the organization. When this is done, the lifetime employment system can become an effective management tool for attaining high productivity.

Three suggestions for achieving high integration are presented: 1) develop a more realistic understanding both by the individual and the organization about the exchange aspect of the career development process under lifetime employment and its potential to foster the individual's passive attitude toward the organization; 2) place more corporate attention on less visible, supportive tasks; and 3) decrease the assignment of employees to tasks that do not allow adequate opportunities to develop necessary task competencies.

First, both the individual and the organization must have mutual expectations for exchange throughout the process of the individual's career development. They must recognize the potentiality that failure in this exchange can lead to an individual's passive involvement in the organization.

Upon entrance to Tokyo Electric, the engineers interviewed had a simplistic expectation that they would be exchanging lifetime employment for long-term loyalty to the company. Corporate management did not communicate its expectation that employees should be willing to continuously strive to acquire new competencies for each task assignment without consideration for individual career preferences. In training and education programs, for example, the company only emphasized the relatively simple philosophy of unity and mutual help among members and expectation for employees' all-encompassing relationships with the organization. Some of the engineers' failure to understand the company's full expectations and to develop necessary competencies has been shown to lead to their essential failure to exchange intrinsic rewards for task accomplishments and develop active member involvement.

This study has demonstrated the usefulness of the general framework in focusing on mutual expectations between the individual and the organization. It has provided the basic factors and patterns of development for active or passive member involvement through successful or unsuccessful exchanges of these expectations. This framework can be recommended for both managers and employees as a diagnostic tool to identify and understand mutual expectations based on specific business and corporate conditions and career development stages. The factors and patterns identified in this book can help locate important exchanges in the process of individual career development and prepare for developing only active involvement.

Furthermore, a better understanding of mutual expectation exchange throughout the career development process can provide a basis for planning certain company programs, such as recruiting, introduction, training and education, and promotion and compensation programs. These programs can be structured around the expectations which are known to be crucial for the development of active or passive member involvement at a particular stage of individual career development. Through these programs, both the organization and the individual can develop a more realistic mutual understanding of and preparation for the exchange of expectations.

A clear understanding of mutual expectations is necessary, but not sufficient to keep employees from becoming passive and to join more passive employees with actively motivated members. In order to optimally attain these goals, managers must strive to correct two fundamental, structural factors in the organization which hinder the individual's exchange of intrinsic rewards for job accomplishments and facilitate the development of passive attitudes toward the organization. They must provide corporate feedback on the accomplishment of less visible, supportive tasks, and they must avoid constantly assigning employees to tasks that do not allow adequate opportunities to develop necessary task competencies.

One of the essential contributors to the development of passive organizational involvement among members is that Tokyo Electric paid only minimal attention to "less important" tasks, even though it had assigned these tasks to its members. Although the results of these tasks usually impacted less visibly and directly on the corporate profits, the effective accomplishment of supportive tasks is definitely necessary to attain corporate goals. The company's minimal attention to these tasks did not recognize employees' contributions or facilitate their exchange of intrinsic rewards for task accomplishments.

Corporate attention to less important task assignments can be increased through both informal and formal means. Informally, managers can give encouragement and support to subordinates through daily leadership activities. In fact, the engineers who were laboratory section managers or department managers with less important tasks often talked to their subordinates about how important these tasks were to the company, and emphasized their subordinates' contributions in corporate business meetings.

However, using only informal means, managers cannot generate as much intrinsic satisfaction for less important jobs as for mainstream tasks.

Therefore, the development and use of a formal system for recognizing contributions from less visible supportive task accomplishments is also recommended.

To my knowledge, no research study has yet been made on a formal management system to recognize contributions from these types of task accomplishments. However, the quality control (QC) circles currently conducted in many Japanese companies provide formal systems of recognition for less important tasks, although more research about the function of these circles is required.

My personal study of Japanese QC circle activities shows that usually fewer than 10 workers in a plant are involved in a QC circle. They focus on problems in their production or service-related jobs, which are the less visible supportive tasks in the company. Once the problem is identified, the circle members study it and suggest and implement a solution. The results of the study and implementation are published in the corporate newspaper, and successful implementation is rewarded in company-wide QC circle conferences. Through this process, the workers develop a sense of importance and worth from their less visible work in the company and increase their motivation and involvement in the organization.

My final suggestion to keep employees from becoming passive and to integrate passive members with actively motivated members is to decrease the assignment of employees to tasks that do not allow adequate opportunities to develop necessary task competencies. Some of the engineers in this study gradually developed passive involvement when they constantly encountered task assignments that did not make use of previously learned skills or help them acquire new competencies. These engineers were never able to receive intrinsic rewards from task accomplishments.

Therefore, this suggestion requires a long-range corporate concern for employees' career development, particularly in the level of difficulty of new task assignments in the company. This can be attained by assessing employee competencies and the difficulty of specific tasks in a personnel planning and development system. Because tasks which are too easy may not interest members, optimum fit between member ability and a task assignment is the key to generating employee intrinsic satisfaction and motivation.

Although it is usually difficult to take individual career preferences into consideration under the conditions of lifetime employment, it is a worthwhile consideration, since its success will help assure high integration between all employees and the organization.

Appendix A

Interview Guide: High-Ranking Manager

1. (Introduce myself and briefly explain the purpose and method of the research. Ensure its confidential nature. All questions were translated into Japanese.)

2. I would like to ask about your organizational unit.
   a. What is the business of this organizational unit? What are the primary concerns in effectively operating the unit?
   b. What are the objectives and goals in your unit? What kinds of reporting systems do you use to monitor how the tasks of this unit are performed?
   c. How precisely do you define job goals and position descriptions in the unit? How do your unit members work together?
   d. What policies do you have for the career development of your members in the unit?

3. Thank you for participating in this interview.

Appendix B

Interview Guide: Research Subject

1. (Introduce myself and briefly explain the purpose of this research. Ensure its confidential nature. Answer any question from the subject. All questions were translated into Japanese.)

2. I'd like to know about your background. What is your educational background? Family background? When did you join this company? Why?

3. I'd like to know what transfers and promotions were turning points of your career from your entry time to the present in the company. Please briefly explain each task assignment which was located between one turning point and another.

4. Now, I'd like to ask about your first task assignment.
   a. Please describe a typical working day in this task assignment. How did you spend free days?
   b. How did you work with other people, such as superiors, colleagues, and subordinates, in the organizational unit?
   c. Were you able to learn how good your job performance was on a daily or weekly basis?
   d. By what aspect of task performance did you feel rewarded? How were you interested in the task?
   e. How easy or difficult was your task assignment? What did you think were your strengths and weaknesses in performing the task?
   f. What was the most difficult period of the task assignment? How did you cope with that difficult period? How did this company help you?
   g. What were the most important aspects of the task assignment to the effectiveness of task performance?
   h. What kinds of reports were required, and how frequently? What kind of job directions did you receive, and how?
   i. What formal or informal mechanisms were used to give you performance evaluation feedback, and how frequently? What did you learn from the evaluation feedback?
   j. How did you feel when you received formal or informal feedback of performance evaluation? How would you have changed the formal or informal feedback mechanisms, so that you could have felt better?
   k. How did you think promotion or salary increase reflected your job performance? How did you feel when you were promoted or received salary increases?
   l. How did the task assignment help increase your skills and abilities? In what areas? Did you feel satisfied with the amount of increase? How about inside or outside training programs which you took, if any?

    m. Did you have a person in this company who was particularly important to your effective task performance and career development during the task assignment? What kind of person? How did you find him? How did he help you?

    n. Did you intend to leave this company during the task assignment? If yes, why? How did you cope with that problem? How did the company help you?

    o. How did the task assignment affect relationships with your family? How did you improve the relationships?

    p. What part of yourself do you think changed during the task assignment? How did you feel about that change?

5. Before proceeding to the next task assignment, I'd like to know about the transition between assignments.

    a. How did you evaluate your initial expectations of your previous task assignment?

    b. When and how did you learn about the decision of your next task assignment? How and how much did you influence that decision?

    c. Was the next task assignment the one which you expected? What was it? How did you feel when you learned about the assignment decision?

    d. How did you expect the next task assignment would influence the development of your career in this company?

    e. How did you intend to utilize experiences in the previous assignment for the next one?

6. (Repeat questions in sections 4 and 5 for all task assignments except for the present one. Use only section 4 for this assignment.)

7. I'd like to ask about your future career expectations in the company.

    a. How do you evaluate your initial expectations of your present task assignment?

    b. What do you expect your next task assignment will be? What kind of information do you want to have for further development of your career in the company?

    c. How do you help your subordinates, if any, perform their jobs effectively and develop their careers in this company?

    d. Is there a person to whom you are becoming important particularly in terms of his job effectiveness and career development? If yes, what kind of person? How do you help him?

8. Thank you for participating in this interview.

Notes

Chapter 1

1. In large Japanese companies, most people are employed for a "lifetime," which means they stay in one company from the time of graduation from high school or university until a mandatory retirement age. The length of the time is usually about 40 years. The term "lifetime employment" is used in this context in this book.

2. In order to clarify the term "integration," I adopted the following definition of integration between the individual and the organization. The definition conceptually underlies this exploratory field research.

    > Integration between the individual and the organization is achieved through the organizational structure and processes when actions of the individual lead to the simultaneous attainment of the organization's objectives and his own.

    "The organization's objectives" mean those qualities that contribute to the creation of its products or the fulfillment of its functions or purposes. The individual's objectives are those that satisfy the needs, motives, or desires of the individual.

    In the definition, I implicitly assume that the organization's objectives are attained by dividing organizational tasks and assigning them to individual members. Each individual must accomplish his task assignment in order for the organization's objectives to be met. If the organizational structure and processes are appropriate, the individual can simultaneously achieve his own personal objectives through the activities which he performs to accomplish his task assignment.

    It should be noted that the individual's and the organization's expectations of exchange for mutual need satisfaction is commonly referred to as "psychological contract" between the two parties in the area of organizational behavior. However, this term is not used here in order to focus more on the development process of integrating relationships between the individual and the organization than on the contract aspect of mutual expectation in this relationship.

3. All organizational, individual, and technological names in this book are fictitious.

Chapter 2

1. A typical example of an organization designed around classical organization theory is a bureaucratic one. Properties of such an organization include the use of technical competence, division of labor and specialization, hierarchy of authority, rules and standard procedures, specification of work duties and authority, recording of all administrative acts, and impersonality.

2.   Human relations theory primarily asserts the following three points: 1) the satisfaction of ego needs and social needs of employees is important to organizational effectiveness; 2) these needs are likely to be satisfied by employee-oriented, group-centered, participative supervision and management; and 3) informal group behavior is essential to improvements in organizational operations.

3.   Motivation-hygiene theory suggests that there is a fundamental difference between the effects that factors such as the job itself, achievement, advancement, and personal growth (motivators) have on human motivation and the effects that factors such as money, supervision, working conditions, and interpersonal relations (hygiene factors) have. Herzberg asserts that the presence of motivators leads to a durable state of motivation, but their absence does not depress motivation, while the presence of hygiene factors does not lead to a durable state of motivation, but their absence can lead to alienation.

Chapter 3

1.   Although the former age period is three years older than Schein's specification for that transition (see chap. 2), Levinson's figures are used in the research because they are based on empirical data.

Chapter 4

1.   The earliest entry year of the engineers interviewed was 1957, and 1982 is the year in which this research was conducted.

2.   Historically speaking, the divisionalized structure was introduced a few years after 1957. In the research, however, only this structure was described. Although some of the engineers interviewed had joined the company a few years before the structural change, their early task assignment situations were hardly affected by the change. Before the change, the manufacturing segment consisted of product departments each of which dealt only with product development and manufacturing, and the marketing segment was composed of marketing planning departments and area sales departments. The divisionalized structure was created through organizationally expanding the product departments to divisions absorbing the marketing planning function from the marketing segment. This segment became composed only of area sales divisions, which were originally the area sales departments.

3.   The periodic recruitment of university graduates started in 1953 while that of the other graduates had begun some years earlier.

4.   The philosophy was established by the founder of Tokyo Industry Co., Ltd., before the creation of Tokyo Electric.

5.   The Department of Human Resource Management dealt centrally with the headquarters-based employees who were placed at the department manager level or below. People above this level were considered by the Board of Directors.

6.   The HRM department partly revised the rank system in 1969. The major point of the revision was the addition of the professional positions at the section and department manager levels. The pattern described in the chapter is revised because most of the engineers interviewed were promoted to section managers or assistant professionals after 1969. Furthermore, the rest, who had been promoted to section managers one or two years before 1969, kept the managerial positions without being transferred to professional ones at the time of the revision.

7. The labels of NMJ1, NMJ2, etc. are for research purposes only. The company had its own formal labels.

8. If a graduate had a master's degree, he would start at NMJ2. If a high school graduate was headquarters-based employed, he would start at NMJ0, which is not indicated in the figure. In the research, there were two subjects with a master's degree, and one subject who was employed after high school graduation and then got a bachelor's degree through evening courses after work. The year each received his bachelor's degree was considered the year of entry into the company.

Chapter 5

1. Levinson (1978) called this age period "age-30 transition."

2. The basic arrangement of this program was established in 1954.

3. It should be noted that in our research subjects there were two engineers who felt more satisfied by the fulfillment of responsibilities than by the verification of strategies. For example, one of them carried out many analytical research and development projects requested by divisions mostly through his assignments in the laboratory. When he established a satisfactory result in such a project and met its deadline, he handed over the result to the client feeling rewarded by the fulfillment of the responsibility. This may imply that there are people who are not primarily motivated and satisfied by the accomplishment of tasks.

4. The actual number of engineers who were transferred based essentially on their wishes before 1966 was not zero. Two engineers were transferred to the research and development laboratory to satisfy their academic interest because they told the supervisors that they were interested in academic job offers from their universities. Another engineer was transferred to a local factory to meet his family needs in that city. However, these are the only examples of individual-triggered transfers in the entire period focused on in this research study.

5. In addition to the planned transfer program, the HRM department established in 1964 the biannual, face-to-face, individual meetings between supervisors and subordinates in order to faciliate their communication. However, my research indicates that the engineers rarely perceived these meetings as effective in getting their career preferences considered in the company.

6. In later years, the company emphasized this policy in advertising for recruitment, stating "Failure is investment for development."

7. There was an exception. One of the engineers was on the executive committee of the union for two years. Through his position and attendance at committee meetings, he received information about personnel administration.

Chapter 6

1. Levinson (1978) called this age period "mid-life transition."

2. The training program for promotion to the section manager level was established in 1969. Four out of the 27 engineers interviewed did not take the program because they had been promoted before its establishment.

3. There was an exception. One of the engineers received the title of assistant professional with managerial responsibility for a sales engineering section in the headquarters. The selection

of either the managerial or professional rank was made by the Department of Human Resource Management.

4. A division group structure was established in 1971. The Lighting Division was then reorganized into several divisions to form the Lighting Division Group. At the same time, the Small Appliances Division Group was created including the Small Appliances Division and some other divisions.

5. In the late 1960s, the company identified the task of product planning as important and established product planning departments and sections. Partly because of this, none of the engineers interviewed experienced the task assignment of product planning during the years focused on in the previous chapter.

6. See n. 4, above.

7. This implies that Levinson's definition of the age period of transition to the mid-career stage is some years later than the promotion to the department manager level of the majority of the engineers. Because these engineers considered this promotion as a substantial turning point of their career development, this transition experience seems to be largely affected by the company's personnel practices.

Chapter 7

1. Laboratory sections and division departments had the same status organizationally.

2. Product departments usually included both product development and production sections in their organization.

Bibliography

Abegglen, J. C. 1958. *The Japanese Factory: Aspects of Its Social Organization.* Glencoe, IL: The Free Press.

Argyris, C. 1964. *Integrating the Individual and the Organization.* New York: Wiley.

Barnard, C.I. 1938. *The Functions of the Executive.* Cambridge, MA: Harvard University Press.

Barrett, J.H. 1970. *Individual Goals and Organizational Objectives: A Study of Integration Mechanisms.* Ann Arbor, MI: Institute for Social Research, The University of Michigan.

Brown, M.E. 1969. "Identification and Some Conditions of Organizational Involvement." *Administrative Science Quarterly* 14:346–55.

Clark, R. 1979. *The Japanese Company.* New Haven, CT: Yale University Press.

Deci, E.L. 1975. *Intrinsic Motivation.* New York: Plenum Press.

Economic Planning Agency (of Japan), ed. 1983. *Handbook of the Economy.* Japan: Printing Division, Ministry of Finance.

Hackman, J.R., and Lawler, E.E., III. 1971. "Employee Reactions to Job Characteristics." *Journal of Applied Psychology, Monograph* 55, 3:259–86.

Hackman, J.R., and Oldham, G.R. 1976. "Motivation through the Design of Work: Test of a Theory." *Organizational Behavior and Human Performance* 16:250–79.

Hall, D.T. 1971. "A Theoretical Model of Career Subidentity Development in Organizational Settings." *Organizational Behavior and Human Performance* 6:50–76.

Herzberg, F. 1966. *Work and the Nature of Man.* Cleveland, OH: World.

Lawrence, P.R., and Lorsch, J.W. 1967. *Organization and Environment: Managing Differentiation and Integration.* Cambridge, MA: Harvard University Press.

Levinson, D.J., et al. 1978. *The Seasons of A Man's Life.* New York: Ballantine Books.

Lorsch, J.W., and Morse, J.J. 1974. *Organization and Their Members: A Contingency Approach.* New York: Harper and Row.

March, J.G., and Simon, H.A. 1958. *Organizations.* New York: Wiley.

Ouchi, W.E. 1981. *Theory Z.* Reading, MA: Addison-Wesley.

Rohlen, T.P. 1974. *For Harmony and Strength: Japanese White-Collar Organization in Anthropological Perspective.* Berkeley, CA: University of California Press.

Schein, E.H. 1971. "The Individual, the Organization, and the Career: A Conceptual Scheme." *Journal of Applied Behavioral Science* 7:401–26.

———. 1978. *Career Dynamics: Matching Individual and Organizational Needs.* Reading, MA: Addison-Wesley.

Takezawa, S. 1975. "Changing Workers' Values and Implications of Policy in Japan." Davis, L.E., et al., ed., *The Quality of Working Life,* Vol. 1. New York: Free Press.

White, R.W. 1963. "Ego and Reality in Psychoanalytic Theory." *Psychological Issues* 3, 33.

Yoshino, M.Y. 1968. *Japan's Managerial System: Tradition and Innovation.* Cambridge, MA: MIT Press.

Index

Abegglen, J.C., 92
Argyris, C., 5-10, 12, 13

Barnard, C.I., 5, 6, 12
Barrett, J.H., 5, 8-9, 12, 13

Career anchor, 15-17
Career development, 10-11
  dynamics of, 14-15, 18-19
  multi-organization, 15
  single-organization, 15
Career issues, 10, 11
Career moves, 10
Career preferences, 47-49, 62-64, 82-83
Career specialization, 32
Career stage, 10-11, 24
  early-, 39-52
  late-, 71-84
  mid-, 53-70
  transition, 10
  turning points, 43, 47, 63
Clark, R., 3
Classical organization theory, 6, 101n1
Compensation, 36-37, 73, 83
Competencies
  human relations, 47, 57, 64-67, 74, 76-77, 81-82
  technological, 49, 64, 67

Deci, E.L., 16

Education programs at Tokyo Electric, 72, 103n2
Exchange
  between the individual and the organization, 85-86
  in activities surrounding the job, 13-14
  in job activities, 13-14
  long-term equity of, 2
  of inducements and contributions, 6
  throughout career development, 94-96

Failures: consequences of, 50-51
Feedback, performance evaluation, 11, 16, 90

Hackman, J.R. and Lawler, E.E., III, 17
Hackman, J.R. and Oldham, G.R., 17
Hall, D.T., 16
Herzberg, F., 8, 14
Human relations competencies. See Competencies
Human relations theory, 6-7, 102n2
Human resources, 11
  management of, 21

Integration, between the individual and the organization
  by accommodation of the organization, 8-10, 13-14
  by exchange of extrinsic rewards, 8
  by exchange of inducements and contributions, 6
  by socialization of the individual, 8, 13
  content of, 14
  context of, 14
  definition of, 101n2
  empirical studies of, 8-10
  exchange aspect of, 2, 13, 89-90. See also Exchange
  Japanese management and, 1-3
  lifetime employment and, 1-3
  literature about, 5-6
  through activities surrounding the job, 14, 16, 18
  through job activities, 14, 16, 18
  through redesigning the organization, 7
Interview guides, 97, 99-100
Interviews, protocol for, 25-28
Intrinsic motivation, 17-18
  intrinsic rewards, 8, 13, 16, 21, 90
Involvement
  active, 66-69, 70, 81-84, 85-89
  passive, 66-68, 70, 81-84, 85-89

Japanese management
  and integration, 1-2
  cultural aspects of, 92-93
  field studies of, 2-3
  "Large Company Disease," 2
  popular belief about, 1
  research about, 92-93
Job opportunities, challenging, 11, 16-17, 86

"Large Company Disease," 2
Lawrence, P.R. and Lorsch, J.W., 8, 9, 24
Levinson, D.J., 19, 24
Lifetime employment, 15
  and human resource management, 39
  and integration, 1-4
  definition of, 101n1
Lorsch, J.W. and Morse, J.J., 5, 8, 9-10, 13, 14, 15, 17-18, 24
Loyalty, 2, 32, 40, 66, 83, 86

"Mainstream" vs. "less important" tasks. *See* Task assignments
Managerial jobs, 35. *See also* Promotion; Transfer
March, J.G. and Simon, H.A., 6
Motivation. *See* Intrinsic motivation
Motivation-hygiene theory, 8, 14, 102n2

Organization climate
  for growth and development, 21
  for job performance, 21
Organization theory, classical, 6, 101n1
Ouchi, W.E., 1-3, 86, 93

Performance appraisal, 35-37, 53-55. *See also* Feedback, performance evaluation
Personality
  adult, 10
  dynamics of, 10
  stable aspects of, 10
Placement, 41-42
Product development and planning. *See* Task assignments
Professional
  assistant, 55
  associate, 73
  principal, 73
Promotion, 33
  decisions, 72
  delay difference, 72
  process, 54, 71-72
  to the department manager level, 66, 71-73
  to the section manager level, 53-57
Psychological contract, 101n2

Psychological energy, 7
Psychological success, 6-8, 16-17, 18
  and organizational effectiveness, 7

Quality control (QC) circles, 96

Recruitment, 32, 39-40
Research method
  longitudinal, 23
  quasi-longitudinal, 23-24
Retirement age, at Tokyo Electric, 32
Rohlen, T.P., 3

Salaries. *See* Compensation
Sales engineering. *See* Task assignments
Same-seniority echelon, 33, 36, 72
Schein, E.H., 5, 10-11, 14, 15-16, 17
Self-actualization, 17
Self-esteem, 16, 18
Seniority, 33, 53-55, 72-73
Sense of competence, 9, 16, 18

Takezawa, S., 2-3
Task assignments, 42
  first-line, 43-44, 46, 49, 68, 74-75
  "less important," 45, 51-52, 56, 61, 64, 68, 74, 81
  Lighting Group Division (Tokyo Electric), 45-46
  "mainstream," 44, 51, 56, 64-66, 69, 74, 81
  product development, 46-47, 61-62, 79-81
  product planning, 59-62, 77-78
  production management, 63
  quality examination, 61, 77-78
  R & D Lab (Tokyo Electric), 43-45
  sales engineering, 45, 58-59, 76-77
  Small Appliance Division (Tokyo Electric), 46-47
  unsuccessful completion of, 50-51
Tatami room, 26
Tenure, 15-16
Theory Z, 2-3, 86, 93
Tokyo Electric Co., Ltd., 23, 29-37, 71
  economic growth, 29-31
  HRM department, 24, 25, 33, 39, 48-49, 54, 72
  human resources, 32
  Lighting Division Group, 24, 25, 31, 41, 45-46, 80, 81
  managerial jobs, 35
  organizational structure, 31
  philosophy, 32
  professional jobs, 35-36. *See also* Professional
  R & D Lab, 24-25, 41, 43-45, 80

ranking system, 33-37
research subjects, 24
retirement age, 32
Small Appliances Division Group, 24, 25,
   31, 41, 46-47, 80, 81
Training programs, 36, 72
Transfer, 42, 47-49

at the department manager level, 80
at the section manager level, 63
planned, 48

White, R.W., 16

Yoshino, M.Y., 2

DATE DUE

GAYLORD			PRINTED IN U.S.A.